Realtactics4disab

Real Tactics for Filing Your Disability Claim

By Tatiana M. Fróes

Copyright © 2018 Tatiana M. Fróes
Realtactics4disabilityclaims.com

All Rights Reserved.

No part of this publication may be reproduced, distributed, or transmitted in any form or by any means, including photocopying, recording, or other electronic or mechanical methods, without the prior written permission of the publisher, except in the case of brief quotations embodied in critical reviews and certain other noncommercial uses permitted by copyright law.

Only Readers with proof of purchase have a limited authorization to make copies of the forms provided. Downloadable materials are for personal use only. Readers are not authorized to share the materials from this book with anyone.

For permission requests, email the author, addressed: "Permission to Use Copyrighted Materials" to realtactics4disability@realtactics4disabilityclaims.com

ISBN: 9781983229398

For errors and omissions, please contact the author at realtactics4disability@realtactics4disabilityclaims.com

Book Cover Designed by Drop Dead Designs
Author Back Cover Image by Peter John Wilson

Disclaimer: I do not present nor intend any materials or topics discussed here to be understood or received or relied upon by readers in any way as specific legal advice, nor as the basis of forming any sort of attorney-client relationship. The ideas and methods that I discuss in these pages are only presented as broadly general to Social Security disability topics, and are not presented nor intended as a substitute for specific legal representation by a disability attorney or other non-legal Social Security disability representative.

I urge all readers of these materials to also please be aware that the materials and topics are general and may not be applicable to all situations nor to any specific reader's claim(s) or situation. While I intend this and all materials I present on this site to be interesting and generally informational, I first and foremost urge all readers of these materials to obtain your own specific legal counsel for your disability claim(s).

Table of Contents

Preface	1
Acknowledgements	5
Tactic 1 – Technical Stuff	9
Reading Assignment for Tactic 1	19
A. How do I know I qualify for disability?	19
Tactic 2 – Timing of Filing	23
Reading Assignment Tactic 2	31
A. Medical Records and Why they matter in a Social Security Claim	31
B. Top 15 Reasons Your Social Security Case Is Being Denied and What to Do Next	37
C. How to Fix Your Medical Treatment and Win Social Security	43
Tactic 3 – Organizing and Reading Your Medical Records	53
Reading Assignment Tactic 3	71
A. Is It Time to Get Rid of Doctor X to Win Social Security?	71

B. Cost Effective Ways to Order Medical Records and Save Money	79
Tactic 4 – The Big Picture and Putting It All Together	85
Tactic 5 – Filing Day!	95
Reading Assignment Tactic 5	111
A. The Social Security Denial Letter: A 'canned' letter?	111
B. Why You Should Immediately Appeal Your Social Security Disability Denial	118
C. How to Balance Your Budget Like A Pro	123
D. How to Create and Maintain a Budget Without Starving	129
Checklist	145

Preface

Congratulations for taking the first step towards your future!

I know filing for Social Security Disability is a big decision. You wish you could work and have a normal life. But life throws you curve balls and now you can't work anymore.

You weigh your options: *Should I file? Should I work part-time? How do I do this?*

While getting disability benefits won't take away the pain and difficulties of managing day-to-day, those benefits will certainly make your financial life a little easier.

Psychologically, having the ability to pay your bills certainly helps those folks who feel like they can't contribute to society anymore (*Psst! You still can!*)

Some thoughts before you start

So now that you have made your decision to file it's time to get everything ready to do so.

Yes, you can simply skip everything and call the Social Security Administration (let's call them SSA) and file your claim right now, but I want you to imagine something for me for a second before you do that:

Imagine you are having fun outdoors and at a certain point a friend of yours tells you to jump off a cliff into the water below. Lots of people are doing it. So why not try? But you've never been in those waters. Sure, it looks exciting and you feel a little daring today. But you hesitate because you also heard of people getting seriously hurt.

You just don't know those waters. You don't know how close the rocks are from the point you are jumping. Jumping may bring a reward but there are also consequences.

Filing for disability is pretty similar.

A lot of people 'jump', (...*i.e.,* file their claim) without thinking or knowing what they are doing. They don't survey the bottom of the water. They don't know where the rocks are. They just jump into filing the claim.

You need to know what you are doing before you file. Survey the waters before you jump. That's what we will be doing on this journey.

The Tactics

The goal of following these tactics is to ultimately file your claim, but not to file right this second. You should not skip steps. Instead, you want to file when you know what you are doing.

No, you will never know as much as a disability attorney does. But you will have a pretty good idea of what you need to do to prepare for the filing, including gathering the right information, knowing if it's the right time to file (so you don't waste your time), and you will also understand a little more what comes next after filing.

All of this in 5 Tactical Steps!

Now, some of the tasks will take some time to accomplish because it may require ordering records from your doctors, but if you have everything on hand you will certainly be able to accomplish it all very quickly and without feeling like you are lost.

If it's too much to do for you because of bad days, *etc.*, that's ok too, because you can always go back to the last task you were working on at your own time.

Finally, if you wish to get some feedback on the tactics and get general questions answered please join the *"Real Tactics For Filing Your Disability Claim" Facebook Group* by typing on your browser **facebook.com/groups/realtactics4filingyourdisabilityclaim/** to join and I will add you to the group!

Pfeew! That was a lot, but we are on our way!

Acknowledgements

This book is the result of many hours of sweat and tears tracking the ins and outs of Social Security Disability claims. But I did not do this alone. My Husband, Paul, was always there to bounce ideas and best practices off of so that you could have the best possible product in your hands. Thank you for your patience and love!

I would also like to thank Hoàng Chi Truong for inspiring me to write this book. I had the honor of working on her lovely memoir *"Tigerfish"* and that opportunity contributed to my desire to write this book.

I also extend a shout out to all my disability attorney colleagues out there who are "in the trenches" and working to bring the best possible result for their clients.

To my readers: I decided that this book should include things that you don't see anywhere else. Most attorneys, rightly so, protect as much of their knowledge as possible. After all, they spent years and years of time and money *"getting good"* at what they do so they can charge for their services and make a living while helping others.

I chose a different path, as a result of many years seeing people come to our firm with absolutely no idea how to start their claim. Some have no idea even why and where you start a claim. Many claimants come to us with the false conviction that if they contributed many years to Social Security, the money is automatically theirs.

The most frustrating part of this process is when people call me wanting to file a claim and they are not even remotely ready to file. In some cases, I have to decline representation because the person has no treatment or believes that because there is a diagnosis they can just use that information and expect to win their claim.

I want to change those notions and give claimants a way to start on the right foot. I want them to know what they should do to get their claim prepared and ready to file. I also want them to have control of their case even if they hire an attorney.

I believe knowledge is key in a better relationship between client and attorney. If the client understands a little more about the process, he or she will be less stressed and therefore, the attorney-client relationship will be much improved.

It is not uncommon for claimants to call Social Security to ask questions about their case and get completely wrong information and then call their attorney and argue that what the attorney is doing is wrong.

But two things are potentially in play here when you call the SSA: the case-worker has no clue about your case and just wants to get off the phone; or has no idea how to answer your question; and the claimant is anxious because he/she doesn't understand the process and he/she prefers to believe a Social Security agent over his/her attorney.

I want that to stop. I want to empower the claimant with knowledge so that the attorney-client relationship is better. The claimant will know what is going on and can actually spend more time concentrating on getting medical treatment and dealing with the medical issues instead of creating more *"monsters in the head"* that really don't exist because they don't understand the process.

This book is dedicated to my husband Paul, whom without I could never be the person I am today. I love you.

Tactic 1 – Technical Stuff

Don't worry! I promise not to put you to sleep with the tech stuff... It can be a tad complicated, but with some close attention, you will rock today's tactic.

Your account with Social Security

This is your first homework.

I know. Nobody likes to do homework, but this is important and there is a good reason to do this before you file.

I want you to type on your browser **www.ssa.gov/myaccount/** and go to the SSA website and create an account.

You don't want to file your case before you create this account (at least not right now).

The reason I want you to open an account with Social Security now (*before filing*) is very simple:

Remember those statements you used to get in the mail every year from Social Security telling you how much you made over the years, *etc.*?

Well, they stopped mailing those statements to taxpayers around 2012, probably to save some trees (*I hope*) and to save the SSA some money of course.

Luckily, however, that statement is now available online and *guess what?* Since you are a great student and you will open that account as part of your homework, you will have access to that same information.

How neat is that?

Very important information to get from the account

Now, why did I ask you to create that account now and to do so before filing your claim?

Simple: for some reason, as soon as you file your claim, *that information seems to disappear from the SSA computers*. I don't know why, it just does. So, try to print or save a copy of the report for future reference.

Here is why the information on the account is important:

1. We are going to need a few pieces of information from that account that is not available anywhere but on that account;

2. The information in the account tells us *if* you can file (*i.e.*, if you qualify), and *how much* you will get if you receive disability benefits or retirement, and some information relevant to *when* you can file.

The first bit of information I want you to look for is your "Principal Insured Amount" or PIA:

The 'Principal Insured Amount' (or "PIA") is simply the amount you would get if you became disabled. That amount tends to be *higher* than the amount you will get for retirement (yes, it can be lower sometimes).

So the first thing I want you to do is to find the PIA on your account.

-You can write it down on my "Super Nifty Checklist" created just for that purpose. To download the checklist please type on your browser **realtactics4disabilityclaims.com/checklist-pdf/** and make copies for your records. Your information goes on the top part of page one of the checklist.

-You should also create a paper file for all the work you will be doing during this challenge and you can save that information there.

Your PIA information is important because it tells you if is worth your time to file your claim.

You may be thinking: *"Why would it be not worth my time?"*

Here are some examples why:

If your PIA is so low that you could make that amount of money or more *'in your sleep'* so to speak, then it's not worth your time filing.

If you're incarcerated, they will not pay you. Wait until you are out of prison to file.

If you are currently receiving unemployment benefits (*while technically you can file, the fact that you are receiving these benefits can severely diminish or negate your claim*).

The second bit of information I want you to get is your *"Date Last Insured"* or DLI:

The date last insured or "DLI" tells us if you are *"insured"* under the system. And when I say insured, I'm saying that it kind of works like a *"premium"* paid to an insurance company.

You may be asking yourself: *"I 'contributed' by paying social security taxes all my life and you are telling me that I may not get my money after all these years?"*

Sadly, I am*.

A few years back the government changed the rule to make it work more like a payment of premium to an insurance company so that if you stop contributing, after about five years, you are no longer "covered" or "insured".

---

* Note that this only applies to disability "coverage". Your money will still be there upon retiring.

So, what do you need to know to see if you're insured under the system and can file now?

To be *"insured under the system"* and get full disability benefits, a person must have worked a minimum of 20 quarters out of the last 40 quarters (approximately 5 years out of the last 10 years) and must have contributed either via W-2 deductions through their employer or paid Social Security taxes via 1099, if self-employed.

I will give you an example: If you stopped working in 2013 and only in 2018 you are trying to file your claim, you may or may not qualify to file for SSDI (or Social Security Disability Insurance).

To qualify, you will have to either file within your DLI or prove that you are disabled before the expiration of your DLI.

Let me give you a visual so you can understand this even better (*it's complicated stuff but you are rocking this!*):

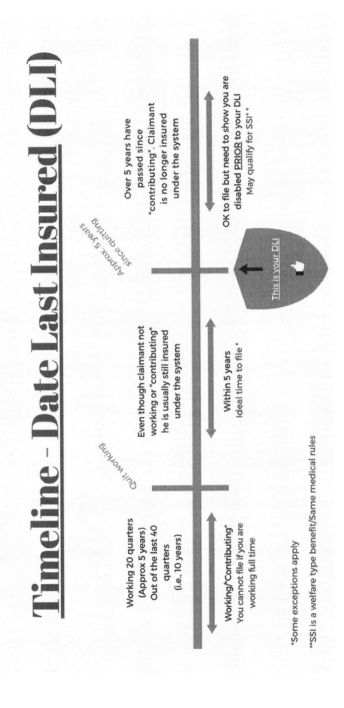

There are some fuzzy areas about this subject that are beyond this publication but the timeline should help in most cases since most claimants will usually file soon after they quit their jobs.

If you fall into a grayer area of the DLI, you should contact an attorney ASAP to figure this out properly.

To recap what we learned so far:

1. You learned about PIA. The PIA tells you how much you will receive each month if you receive disability benefits. And that information tells you if it's even worth filing your claim.

2. You learned about DLI. The DLI tells you if you can file (*i.e.*, if you qualify to file) and when to file.

The Alleged Onset Date (or "AOD")

The "Alleged Onset Date" or "AOD" is simply the date you believe you became disabled. The AOD is not necessarily found in the account you just opened but a lot of the information found there tells us when filing is a good idea (*when your income stopped, or your DLI*).

For more examples of how the AOD affects your ability to file, take a look at your reading assignment **A. How to Know if You Qualify for Disability-Part 1** (at the end of this chapter on page 19 – Reading Assignment for Tactic 1).

Important things to know about the AOD:

1. The AOD, in most cases, coincides with the date people stopped working:

    For example, Claimant had a heart attack on January 1, 2015. He was still employed but never went back to work. His AOD will be January 1, 2015.

2. The AOD can be a little *fuzzier* when you have a deteriorating medical condition that you really don't have a specific date for when it began.

    In this case, you will still use the date you stopped working:

    For example, Claimant has Fibromyalgia. She has been working for years with the condition, but the symptoms finally got so bad that she had to stop working. The AOD will be the date the person last worked even though the condition began sometime in the past.

3. The AOD may have to be a selected date that does not coincide with the last date worked:

    For example, Claimant stopped working 4 years ago due to a medical condition. He never filed until now. He could allege the date he last worked 4 years ago but Social Security will pay benefits going back only *one year* prior to filing if the person has an older AOD like in this example. Essentially, it's a regulatory limiting of the AOD for your case.

Tactic 1 – Technical Stuff

4. The AOD may have to be selected from a date coinciding with when the medical records became *"better"* in reporting the claimant's impairments:

    For example (and this happens a lot), the claimant became disabled in 2013 but he never saw anyone other than a primary physician during that year and the records from that doctor are not that good in reporting the medical issues of that claimant.

    The Claimant finally gets a referral to a specialist who prescribes a bunch of tests and films to see what he/she can do to help the claimant. Finally, one of the films along with the medical treatment shows severe impairments in 2014. The date of that film (2014) can be used as the AOD since that's the time when you can actually prove you are disabled.

    This scenario is most commonly seen in court or when you have an attorney who knows that by changing the AOD you will have a more solid case for the judge.

5. Occasionally, the local Social Security office will award cases and change the AOD for some or all the reasons we've just talked above, though they are not always clear in explaining this to you. A lot of people get confused when that happens, but unless you have very solid medical records to show an earlier AOD, one should really consider whether it is wise to appeal that decision[†]

[†] Case by case, please. Don't take this as a the only possible answer in your particular case-Find an attorney to check if the amended AOD is fair.

Final thoughts on Tactics 1

Pfeew! ... That was a lot of information to learn but you did it! This information is very technical, and you are probably wondering why you are learning this. But I hope you understand that by learning this you are light years ahead of anyone filing on their own. You are also starting to get a big picture of your case.

So in Tactic 1, you gathered your PIA, DLI and AOD. In Tactic 2, we will get to work on the timing of the filing based on your medical records.

Congratulations on completing Tactic 1!

Reading Assignment for Tactic 1

A. How do I know I qualify for disability?

The first thing people wonder when they get sick or injured is whether they qualify for disability.

How long is your sickness or injury going to last?

No matter what type of disability you are applying for you must ask yourself: *Is this temporary?* If so, for how long? *Will it last 3 months? 6 months? 12 months?* Or years into the future?

Is the disability the result of an injury? Will it take a while to heal but eventually get better? Or is it a medical condition or injury that medical science has not been able to cure yet?

The answer to these questions is a good way to start in deciding when and if you should file for disability.

The time consideration is important because if you are applying for Social Security, the rules require you to demonstrate that *the disability will last or is expected to last more than 12 months.*

Very Important: The clock (for receiving disability) starts ticking not from when you first became injured or sick (*although it's important*) but when you stopped working. This date is the so-called ONSET DATE, i.e., the date your disability began.

Yes, sometimes those two (became sick/stopped working) coincide on the same date.

For example, you had a car accident on January 1st, 2015 and you stopped going to work after that day. But then there is also the issue of when the actual payments begin: a lot of people get injured or sick and they file the very next day thinking that the payment of their benefits will start immediately.

But that is not the case. *EVER!*

Even if by some miracle you get approved right away, there is another little rule that you must consider: the *"5 month-waiting rule"*

The *"Five month-waiting"* rule means that even if you win your disability right away, you will still have to wait *Five fully elapsed months* from the date you were found to be disabled to get paid. Realize also that they will not pay you retroactively for those 5 months you waited[‡].

[‡] This rule applies for SSDI only. SSI payments start as soon as you are awarded.

For example, you filed your disability on January 2, 2015, and you receive your award letter soon after. The benefit payments will only start 5 months *after* January 2, 2015.

Another example, if you filed on January 2, 2016, and you received your award letter in May 2016 (*i.e.*, a year and four months *after* your initial onset date of January 2, 2015). In this scenario, Social Security will *deduct* five (5) months of benefits. This means that your back-pay check for the future months starting from January 2015 will only include 11 Months of benefits instead of 16 months. In other words: January 2015 thru May 2016 = *16 months* minus *5 months* = *11* months of benefits included in your back-pay.

Is There Such a Thing as a Temporary or "Short Term" Social Security Disability Benefit?

Some claimants think that Social Security has a mechanism similar to the so-called *"short term disability"* plans (*disability insurance through an insurance company*) and that SSA will pay temporary benefits while you are sick until your return to work. While under the rules there is such a benefit, it doesn't always work that way.

There is a mechanism in the Social Security rules providing for something similar to short term disability, but you still have to meet the *12-month rule* we talked about above. Also, the payment is not as immediate as you think.

Because of the application process, the time it takes to get a response and the deduction of the 5 months, by the time you get awarded anything you are back to work already. So, any payments would be retroactive, and they would not take care of you during the time you were sick.

Also, in most cases, Social Security takes advantage of the idea that this is temporary and hopes you give up waiting so that they don't have to pay for that period. Further, they can keep denying temporary benefits, and the fight to get just a few months of coverage is really not worth the trouble. Social Security is counting on that. So, while some people try the claim usually doesn't go that far.

To recap:

1. Ask yourself if your condition has *lasted or is expected to last 12 months or more* before you consider filing for disability;

2. Understand that the clock for setting your alleged onset date starts ticking from the time you stopped working;

3. Social Security will not pay for the first 5 months after your awarded onset-date even if you are awarded right away;

4. "Short Term" Social Security sort of exists but you still need to meet Rule Number 1. *Is it worth the trouble?*

Tactic 2 – Timing of Filing

How Do You Feel So Far?

Just a recap:

Before you started the challenge you opened an account with Social Security. And we talked about PIA (Principal Insured Amount), DLI (Date Last Insured), and AOD (Alleged Onset Date).

You should pat yourself on the back. This is stuff that most people who are filing will never know or understand. You not only know what these terms mean but you also know how significant they are for your claim.

So,... Yay to you!!

Tactic 2 is About the Timing of Filing

You are probably thinking: *"But we already covered that on Tactic 1 with all the DLI and AOD stuff. What now?"*

Remember I told you that Tactic 1 was all about the technical stuff? Well, that technical stuff told us about the timing of the filing but in an *"administrative"* setting.

Tactic 2 and 3 is all about whether you *can* or *should* file your claim based on your "medical treatment and medical records".

But before we get to Tactic 2, I want to go over one more thing that gets people confused: The difference between **SSDI** (or Social Security Disability Insurance) and **SSI** (or Supplemental Security Income).

We all hear the two terms (*SSI and SSDI*). People often use them interchangeably, thinking that they mean the same thing.

They don't!

The only rules that are the same for both terms are the medical rules for when it's time to file for disability and for what medical evidence is deemed sufficient to win. Otherwise, they are very different from one another.

SSDI

The name kind of says it all: *Social Security Disability Insurance*. Another name for it is Title II (*it is found under Title 2 of The Social Security Act*) if you want to get fancy.

Remember yesterday when we talked about *"contributions"* and *"premiums"*, much like with an insurance company policy?

Well, SSDI is a benefit that you get only if you have *contributed* to the system through paying taxes and you have filed your claim within the time-frame of your DLI (*i.e., proven you were disabled before the expiration of your DLI*). If you did not contribute to the system or your DLI expired long before you filed, expect your SSDI claim to be denied for those reasons.

Most people WANT to file for SSDI because it usually (*not always*) pays you more money than SSI.

Of course, wanting SSDI does not mean you can get it. If you don't qualify "procedurally" based upon what we talked about yesterday (DLI, AOD, *etc.*), then you may only have one more option: *SSI*.

SSI

SSI or Supplemental Security Income is exactly what the name says: *Supplemental Income*.

It usually doesn't pay as much as its cousin SSDI. Also, with SSI the AOD and DLI are not much of a concern.

SSI is pretty much a federal welfare benefit and its fancy name is Title XVI of The Social Security Act (*that's Title 16 if you can't remember Roman numerals*).

In most cases, claimants file for SSI if their DLI has expired or they have not paid taxes into the system long enough to accrue adequate quarters for insured status. The idea is that the SSA wants to make sure everybody has at least something to live on if they get sick, blind or reach retirement age.

However, there is one very big issue when applying for SSI: **Your current financial situation.**

If you have no income source at all or live with a spouse or family member who doesn't make too much money, in most cases, you should be able to file for SSI.

Things get more complicated when the claimant is married and the spouse makes money above the *income limit* established by the SSA. Or the claimant has other assets that are considered *"excessive"* for purposes of filing (*like life insurance policies, etc.*).

I won't get into too much detail here because this is a very complex area to get into. Just know that there is a *financial* threshold you cannot go over in order to qualify for SSI.

If you feel ambitious enough you can read more about it at **www.ssa.gov/pubs/EN-05-11015.pdf**. It is not required reading for this publication unless you think you fit the description of a claimant who should be filing for SSI. In that case, the best way to know if you qualify for SSI is to actually file the claim.

But that doesn't mean you should not continue with our tactics since there is still work to do for your claim to be in good shape for a win.

...Well, enough about technical stuff. *Let's get to work!*

How Can My Medical Treatment Tell Me When to File My Claim?

I cannot emphasize enough how important your medical treatment and your medical records are for winning a disability claim.

I wrote quite a few articles about medical records (and how important they are for your claim) on my blog

Realtactics4disabilityclaims.com, but I want you to read two of these articles very carefully as part of today's tactics, even if you've read them before:

1. **Medical records and why they are so important:** this article talks about the importance of the medical records in your claim; and 2. **How to fix your medical records.** The articles can be found at the end of this Chapter on page 31 – Reading Assignment Tactic 2).

As you read the articles, I want you to think about your own medical treatment. Then after you read the posts, I want you to write about your medical treatment. You may add that information on page two of the Checklist you downloaded (or you can use a piece of paper if you don't have a printer).

The list should include the name of your doctors, their addresses and phone numbers, their specialty (*primary, endocrinologist, etc.*) and what he/she is treating you for (*Diabetes, Heart, etc.*).

This list will give you an idea if you are treating with the right medical providers.

You may be thinking, "*How is having the name and address of my doctor telling me whether I'm getting the right treatment?*"

I know that addresses and names will not give you much other than the fact that you will need that information when it's time to file. But don't think you are wasting your time with that. In fact, all that work will come in handy before and after the filing.

Now, the part where you list the specialty and what the doctor is treating you for,... *that's where the gold mine is!*

So even though you spent some time writing names and addresses (*yes, I know that part was boring*), this will pay off for you in the end because now you will be ready for the filing. But you are also getting a "big picture" of what your treatment looks like.

For example, you may realize after writing the names down, that you have a medical condition that is very serious but that's not getting any attention from you or a doctor. Or you may realize that your serious medical condition is being treated by a nurse when (*at least according to the SSA*) you really should be seeing a specialist (a doctor).

See how that works?

You may also list *all* your medical conditions on that list and see which medical conditions (*the very serious and debilitating ones*) are not being treated at all. Either because you don't have the time, the money or you are concentrating on one condition only.

It is important to know what condition(s) is/are not getting any attention so you can figure out what to do next (*more treatment, change doctors, etc.*).

I promise it will all make sense in the end. And remember that with what you are learning here you are still *light years* ahead of most claimants filing today!

To recap Tactic 2:

- **SSDI:** those benefits available for those who *"contributed"* to Social Security by paying taxes for five of the last ten years that they worked.

- **SSI:** welfare-type benefits for those who did not have enough tax contributions and/or their DLI expired long before filing, or homemakers and others who never worked at all, or those who are at retirement age.
- **The importance of Medical Records** for the claim. Your reading assignment about the subject and you made a list of all the doctors and what they are treating you for.

That was a lot! But you did great!

Don't worry if it takes you longer than you expected to do this task. Take two days if you must. Some of you will need to take breaks or will need to take some time to get the information for the checklist. …*It's OK!*

What matters is that you work on this at your pace and don't give up.

The next Tactic is an interesting one and quite valuable for your case:

You will learn how to read a medical record with the eye of a disability attorney. You will learn what we attorneys look for in the medical records when we are evaluating a case.

And if you decide to hire an attorney, later, your preparation will pay off *"Big Time"*.

I will explain more in Tactic 3.

And if you have any questions about Tactic 2, you can post them in the Facebook Group.

Reading Assignment Tactic 2

A. Medical Records and Why they matter in a Social Security Claim

Your medical records are a vital part of your disability claim. Without them, you have nothing!

I mean, *nothing*.

In part one of my article about **15 reasons why people get denied disability** (your next reading assignment on page 37), we talk about how a high percentage of cases are denied *"just because…"* (*well, they kind of hope you give up and go away*)

Today we will talk about a very interesting reason that people get denied.

I say interesting not because it's interesting to see people getting denied. The reason I say interesting is because it is surprising how many people don't know how important their medical records are when they are applying for disability.

I get calls every day from people wanting to apply and when I ask them what kind of treatment they are getting they say: "I haven't seen a doctor in 3 years"! That means this person's records are at least 3 years old! *That's a huge gap in treatment, and moreover the records for those three years are pretty much the only records the government is really interested in!*

Now, here's my question: *"If you are not treating, how do you know you are disabled?"*

Better yet, if you think you are disabled, *"how do you expect to prove that you are if you have not seen a doctor in years?"*

What if your condition is treatable and the treatment can get you back to normal? And if it's disabling, *how do we know how disabling your condition is if you are not seeing a doctor?* This is certainly what the government will be wondering.

I also get claimants whose doctors have given up or told them: *"There's not much we can do for you."* The claimant then gave up treatment because of those words and threw their hands in the air in frustration.

Doctors are wrong all the time, often just because the medical establishment can be pretty rigid in their approach!

Yet the good news is that science gets better all the time. There is almost always a treatment, there is almost always something that can be done to alleviate symptoms: *coping mechanisms, therapy, etc.*

For example, we are now learning that there is a cure for Hepatitis C. This was not available just a few years ago.

How cool is that?!

Even in those situations where the doctor said, "*Nothing can be done anymore*," claimants should still find some kind of treatment such as *pain management, aqua therapy, some maintenance appointments* at least.

And if your condition is one that there is *really* nothing your doctor can do for you other than managing it (*pain management, therapy*), you should get a letter from that doctor, so he can explain to Social Security *why* there is nothing he can do for you.

What you *can't do* is not see a doctor for a long period of time and expect that Social Security awards your case.

Here is a big secret about that:

Social Security Sees No Treatment as Improvement!

In other words, they think that if you are not going to the doctor your condition must be "*not that bad*"! Simple as that!

Here's another kicker:

Diagnosis alone will not win cases!

The biggest mistake claimants make is thinking that just because they received a diagnosis they can win a disability claim.

Wrong!

Diagnosis is only the beginning.

People have heart attacks and go back to work. People have cancer and go back to work. These are very serious diagnoses but with the right treatment and time, a lot of people are able to go back to work.

And remember, some claimants may not be able to do the work they used to do but *they may be able to do something else.*

That's why medical records are so important. Once you receive a serious diagnosis, the next step is *treatment*.

Treatment will generate more medical records. More medical records generate a big picture of how disabled you are.

What exactly are medical records?

I'm sure you know what they are, but sometimes I get people who don't know the difference, *so here it goes*:

Medical records are doctor's notes, reports from tests, lab results and anything that has to do with your medical treatment.

Every time you go to a doctor's appointment your doctor usually takes notes of all his/her findings. He/she will also note your complaints during their examination. It is those notes that are *so important*. Every time you get a CT or an X-ray, the clinic generates a report and a film.

These notes and reports are what Social Security is looking for.

Medical Records versus Patient Instructions

Now sometimes, you go to a hospital and the hospital will give you papers containing information about your diagnosis. You also get a list of things you should or shouldn't do after being discharged from the hospital. These look the same for all patients. These are not your actual medical records. These are called *patient instructions*.

They *can* be submitted with the records when you file your case. But *they are not* very useful for your claim. A lot of people get these confused with their *"real"* records and submit these instruction sheets as evidence of disability.

Like I said before, *they don't help that much, if at all.*

Gathering Medical Records

What I want you to do from now on is this:

Every time you go to the doctor *or* every so many months of visits, ask for a copy of your records.

In my State (*Arizona*), people are legally entitled to a copy of their medical records (*please check your jurisdiction*).

There is an exception for mental patients who are a danger to themselves or others. In these cases, doctors fear the person may harm himself/herself if they see what the notes say. Doctors may only release them to a trusted family member and for a particular purpose (*like hiring an attorney or a new doctor*). Either way, *you should ask for them.*

The reason I'm suggesting that you ask for your records is simple: While Social Security will order medical records in the *early* stages of your case, they will not share them with you or your attorney at that stage.

Most attorneys will ask to see your records *before* they decide if they will take your case. The reason is mostly because attorneys need to see if you are getting the right treatment and whether your records show any indicia that you are disabled before taking your case.

Without seeing these records, it is very difficult for an attorney to assess your chances at winning your claim.

The only time Social Security will share a copy of your medical records is the final stage when your case is on the hearing track.

Even then, you will need to request those records before an attorney decides to represent you since they only release these records to the attorney of record (*i.e., after* the attorney decided to represent you).

To Recap:

1. Medical Records are key for the success of your claim;

2. Treatment is a generator of medical records;

3. Social Security thinks if you are not seeing a doctor your condition is *"not as bad"* as you say;

4. Ask your doctor for copies of your medical records to keep track of your treatment.

B. Top 15 Reasons Your Social Security Case Is Being Denied and What to Do Next

People get denied disability benefits every day. But do they really know *why* they got denied?

Some claimants are certain they will win their case simply because they have a diagnosis and they feel they can't work anymore.

Few think about *what it takes* to win a case and many think that if *"the neighbor got disability benefits and I see him moving around just fine, I should too."*

Today, I will be giving you the top 15 reasons people are denied disability benefits.

Important: This list is *not* foolproof or exclusive. There are many other reasons people get denied.

This list is not limited to those reasons you will see in the denial letter, which is more specific to each person's case. What I am listing here today is basically the *"background"*, the *"backstage"* or what *went on in the mind* of the "decision maker" when he/she decided to deny your case.

Here it goes:

1. *"I am going to deny this claimant 'just because'"* ...i.e., A high percentage of cases are denied in the first round! Sad but true. But consider this denial as part of "the game".

2. Your medical records may not describe your conditions very well.

   I'm not talking about the diagnosis listed in the records or the part where you describe how you feel. I'm talking about the *objective examination* conducted by your doctor. What your doctor actually describes when he examined you.

3. You are not receiving the right treatment(s) for your condition(s). You may have been denied simply because you may not be seeing the right type of doctors.

   Other times people concentrate on one medical issue and see only one specialist. They forget all other impairments and yet list all these impairments in their application without seeing doctors for them.

   Another issue with doctors that I see all the time, which most people don't know: Treating with a primary physician alone will *rarely* win cases no matter how well intended and qualified your primary physician is.

4. Your records are too old, and you are not seeing doctors now.

   A lot of people file thinking that their diagnosis and records from 3 years ago will be sufficient to win their case. It doesn't work that way. *You need to be treating right now!*

5. Diagnosis alone does not win cases.

I get this one a lot. People get diagnosed with something serious (for *e.g., heart attack, cancer*) and because of this diagnosis, they think they can win right away.

A lot of these diagnosed conditions are serious, and some people will never work again because of them. But you need to realize that people have heart attacks every day and eventually they go back to work. People have cancer and go back to work.

It may take a little while, but they go back to work.

This is the very reason why the "decision maker" wants to know about your treatment ...*not* just the diagnosis. The overall treatment records can tell them if you are disabled "*permanently*" or not.

6. You think you are disabled under the rules, but you are not.

    Social Security only needs to show that you can do *some other job* than the one you can't do anymore, and case closed.

7. Your doctor may not be supporting the notion that you are disabled. Either because they are unsure how the process works, or the doctor simply doesn't believe in disability (*it happens more often than you think*).

8. Some of your treatment may be a violation of the rules. I know, it sounds weird but it's true. There are medical treatments that violate the rules. *E.g., medical marijuana.*

While it is legal in some States, it's not yet legal in the federal system (*The Social Security System, for example, is federal*).

Unfortunately, medical marijuana treatment still carries an *"illegal drug"* stigma and it can hurt your case.

9. Your case is less than sympathetic because your behavior may be causing the impairment or making it worse.

    Illegal drugs are a pretty obvious one but what if you are smoking when you have lung issues, or drinking when you have cirrhosis or hepatitis?

    The list goes on.

    The decision maker may feel *"less sorry"* for you simply because, despite a serious condition, you are still doing the one thing you shouldn't be doing for a person with your medical issue.

10. Procedurally, you don't qualify, or you need to overcome a *"remote onset"* of disability.

    This is a big one. It means that if you haven't worked in years (more than 5) you may not qualify for benefits because you are no longer insured under the system.

11. It's too early to file. You need to show that your condition has *lasted or is expected to last twelve months or more*.

12. Anger issues and bad attitude shown in your medical records.

In mental disability cases, certain behaviors are expected because people are not in their best mental shape. Now, in physical cases *(bad back, heart problems etc.)*, that's a *no-no!*

Do not throw tantrums at your doctor's office.

A lot of times doctors will write that in their notes and the "decision maker" will see it.

Instead, try to control your anger when you are at your doctor's office, so that your doctor writes more sympathetic content. No matter how objective the decision maker is supposed to be, he/she is still a person, and people tend to connect with the *"underdog"* or the ones *"who are suffering."* It may help if the decision maker sees you as that *underdog*.

Don't ruin that by being a *jerk* at the doctor's office no matter how wrong the doctor or staff is!

13. Incarceration.

    You can't get benefits while incarcerated. *Simple as that.* Wait until you're out.

    They will not pay for the period you were incarcerated even if you qualify for it medically *during* the time of incarceration.

14. Faking Disability:

    This one really gets me. People sometimes call and say they are disabled and they are all mysterious about their medical condition, but they want to hire a lawyer to *"fight for them"*.

They present some records to show there is a diagnosis and think that's enough. They talk about the neighbor getting disability and think they should get it too, and thinking that just because they hired a lawyer, things will magically happen. *They don't!*

Attorneys and "decision makers" in Social Security and private insurance companies can spot fakers in seconds! *"Fakers"* are the reason it's so hard to win disability these days.

Just don't even try!

15. You're receiving Unemployment Benefits:

    Yep, I know you need money during the pendency of the disability case, but the sad reality is this: *if you are receiving unemployment your case will be denied* or *your benefits will be offset by your unemployment benefits* during the time you were receiving those unemployment benefits. While the rules allow people to receive unemployment and apply, the reality is very different.

C. How to Fix Your Medical Treatment and Win Social Security

We talked a lot about medical treatment and medical records in my article about the **15 reasons people get denied Social Security**.

Today we are going to talk about medical treatments and why they are so important.

We will also talk about why your medical treatment may be the real reason your claim was denied.

Your medical treatment is the most important thing to concentrate on if you are planning to file for disability or you have an ongoing claim.

But what is considered medical treatment?

You are probably thinking: *"well, medical treatment is simply going to the doctor and getting some medications, so I can feel better."*

Perhaps. But there is more to it than just going to the doctor and getting medication.

Medical treatment is also going to the RIGHT doctor and getting the RIGHT treatment

I get calls every day where claimants tell me they are going to the doctor for treatment. But when I ask more details about what kind of doctors they are seeing they tell me that they are seeing one doctor.

In most cases, *a primary physician, a nurse, a physician's assistant or a chiropractor.*

I also get those claimants who tell me they have 5 serious medical conditions but are only dedicating their time to one or two of them. Others call me and tell me that they are not getting ANY medical treatment but want to file based on a diagnosis they received 2 or 3 or 4 years ago.

Finally, I get the ones that just recently received a diagnosis, or just got out of the hospital and have yet to go for a follow-up appointment to start treatment.

All of these claimant's cases suffer from one basic problem: They ALL lack the RIGHT medical treatment to support their disability claim

You ask:

"How do you know this without even seeing what my records look like?"

"What if my primary doctor or my nurse says I'm disabled? Shouldn't Social Security believe my doctors or nurses?"

"Why would my doctors lie if they didn't believe I am disabled?"

In an ideal world, yes: Social Security should believe your doctor when he says you're disabled.

But *doctors are wrong quite often*. And sometimes doctors are just trying to get to the next patient and they agree to fill out any forms just to get you out of their room.

Judges know that!

Finally, there is one thing that most doctors don't know, and that is the critical importance in the disability world of the difference between not being able to do the job you used to do, and not being able to do *any* job: ...*i.e., you may not be able to do your old job but what if you can do some "other job".*

Your doctor may say you're disabled because he/she believes you shouldn't be a truck driver anymore. But doctors usually don't understand the disability claim process, and probably do not know that to win you must show the inability to do *any* jobs.

Only by asking your doctor, point blank, "*can I do any other job?*" can you really know for sure whether your doctor is fully in support of your disability claim

Many doctors when posed with this question, may say: "*Yeah, I think you can do something else.*" But most people don't ask that question or just don't want to hear the answer.

So, if your question to your doctor about whether you are disabled focuses only on the physical requirements of your own profession you are *not* getting the real answer.

Again, remember that Social Security only needs to find some other job (*in theory*) that you can do, and your claim is over. I know you feel sick and you probably want to just rest. But you really need to ask this question:

"Do you think I can sustain work in any type of full time jobs at all?"

Better yet, what you really should ask is: *"From what you can tell right now, are my working days as a full-time worker over?"*

You will only be fooling yourself in going forward with your claim if the answer to your question is *NO*. Imagine your time wasted and your anxiety going through the process of defending your claim while not knowing the answer to this question, until maybe it is too late to get the claim back on track.

Why am I telling you this? *"I just don't want you to waste your time if the claim is not currently supportable!"*

Life is already hard enough!

In a nutshell, if you are perceived as having the ability to sustain working some other full-time job, even if you are not trained to do another job, and even if it doesn't pay as well as your old job, *you simply do not qualify for disability under the social security regulations.*

If you might not qualify for disability in the first place, you really need to take as early a look as possible at your impairments, so you don't waste two or more years of your life going through the stress of pursuing a losing claim.

This is not an easy ride. I promise you!

It breaks my heart to see someone calling me after years and years pursuing their claim and when I ask them if they could do some other job, and they hesitantly say *"Yeah, I never really thought about it that way, I guess I could"*.

They just wasted their time.

If only they knew about this crucial detail before they filed their claim…

The Right Doctors

Earlier in this book we had clarified why Social Security might not believe your doctor at first; now we need to go over why seeing certain other types of medical professionals aside from your doctors can also hurt your claim. I'm talking about nurses (RNs, LPs), Physician's Assistants (PAs), Licensed Social Workers and Chiropractors.

I'm not saying these other types of medical practitioner don't have the competency to make medical assessments. They do! And sometimes they do a better job than doctors!

But the issue here is *"weight"* of the evidence.

What is that? Evidence does not need to go on a diet. In fact, the *"heavier"* the better!!

…And I am only partly joking.

Evidence has *"weight"* when it carries *"credibility"*. For our purposes credibility comes from *"credentials"*. …Credentials in this case come with an *M.D* or *D.O* or *Ph.D*. after the name.

It's that simple.

In other words: **It doesn't matter that you have the best nurse in the world! "Heck, I love my nurse!"**

But when it comes to taking your case to court, a judge will be looking for *those credentials*.

A nurse is always seen as someone who takes care of the *"sniffles"* even if it's not true! Imagine how many lives were saved because nurses were checking vitals, medications, and were otherwise in the right place at the right time!

But unfortunately, we live in a society that still sees a practitioner's place in this medical *"pecking order"* as a true indicator of knowledge and credibility.

That doesn't mean your nurse's records won't carry some weight. Especially if she/he is understood to be supervised by an *M.D.*, and also has been treating you for years.

But for a disability claim, especially Social Security, you will need an *M.D. "running the show"*. And not just any *M.D.*, ...*an M.D. specialist!*

Which takes us back to the start of our conversation: The RIGHT medical people!

So, hopefully you have an *M.D. "running the show"* like I suggested, but you should still consider: *"Is my doctor enough to support my claim?"*

If all you have is a family physician, the answer may very well be "No!

Why?

Because the function of a family physician is to treat most *"minor"* medical conditions. "Maintenance" is a good word. Like your "tune-up" doctor. The one who *"changes the oil and rotates the tires"*, so to speak.

"Why am I describing your family doctor like this?" Because that is how they are too often seen in the disability world.

I know that diabetes or high blood pressure are serious conditions, and indeed these are things most family doctors competently treat, but if you have a bad back, or if your diabetes is out of control, or if your heart requires more than just a high blood pressure medication, you really, really should be seeing *a specialist*.

In fact, if you are a person that needs to focus on your most serious medical conditions because your finances are constrained by financial concerns, such as insurance co-pays, then concentrate on your impairments that require a specialist; those will be your most serious conditions.

If you have sinus problems, for example: yes, you will have pain and discomfort, but these are almost always *not disabling* under the social security rules. So, leaving the sinus problem to a family doctor is fine.

But if you have a serious heart condition, please see a *Cardiologist*!

If, despite trying all sorts of medications, your diabetes is out of control, go see an *Endocrinologist*!

If you have a bad back, go see an *Orthopedist or a Spinal Surgeon*. Just pain pills from your family doctor will not win a disability case.

A specialist doctor carries a lot of *"weight"* when it comes to supporting a claim. A lot!

When judges look at a claim, they want to know that the doctors treating you are specialists in their fields.

These doctors have studied their particular specialty for years. A family doctor is not enough to win cases for this reason:

They usually know a little about everything, but quite often not in great detail, and not in depth like a specialist does.

And because *your specialist* knows his field of practice really well, the judge at least will know, that your doctors, as specialists, were much more likely to have tried everything medically available to treat you and cure you.

Specifically, if despite all specialty treatment you are *still* not cured, and to all indication may never be, a judge will have a pretty good idea that *you really are disabled*.

...or at least, that's what you aim for when you bring medical records from a specialist.

Ok, so, let's assume you are now seeing a specialist; the next question becomes:

"How do I ensure my medical treatment is sufficient to improve my chances at winning my case?"

First, your homework after reading this section will be to make a list of your medical conditions and answer this one question honestly for each of those conditions:

"Does this impairment alone prevent me from working?"

If the answer is *"yes"*, get a specialist *M.D.*, (or *D.O.* or *PsyD*) and start treating with him or her now!

And if you already have a specialist for that particular condition, *then good for you!*

You are on the right track!

If the answer to the question is *"no"* on the other hand, (that is, you could work full-time despite that condition: *e.g.,* sinus, controlled diabetes, mild carpal tunnel, *etc.*), then you can rely on your family doctor for those lesser conditions.

So, in sum, where appropriate, you should consider getting a specialist to add *"weight"* to your evidence: The more *"weight"* your evidence has, the better.

So why not?

And I know money is sometimes a consideration when deciding to go to a specialist. But without one, *it will be very difficult to win your claim.* So, if you are in a limited financial situation then *at least* narrow down to the most serious conditions that you have and get a specialist, or specialists for those. Then your family doctor can take care of the rest.

To recap:

1. What kinds of doctors are treating your medical conditions?

2. Are they specialists?

3. List your medical conditions and ask: *Does this condition alone prevent me from working?* If so, then get a specialist for that condition.

Tactic 3 – Organizing and Reading Your Medical Records

First of all, I'm very proud of you! You have done amazing things in the past few days.

You opened an account with SSA. You learned about "PIA", "DLI", and "AOD". You also learned about the importance of your medical records for your claim and learned how to fix some of the issues with your treatment.

Today, you will learn how to read your medical records like a pro!

I will also give you a window into what attorneys are looking for when they evaluate a claim to see if they will take a case.

Why is all of that important?

...because eventually you are going to want an attorney to represent you (*you really should get one from your State*), and you need to know what to do to improve your chances so that an attorney *will want* to take your case.

I know what you are thinking: *"You are telling me that not only do I have to prepare my case to win Social Security but I also need to improve my records to be accepted by an attorney?*

Yes! That's exactly what I'm saying.

Here's why:

Unless it's one of those big law firms that are only interested in numbers and will take anything that walks in the door, if an attorney takes your case that means there is a good possibility it's a good case.

In a way, it's a *thermometer* for your case.

Now, just because an attorney is interested in your case, it doesn't mean it's a *"slam-dunk"* case, or that there isn't work to be done to improve it. *But it's usually a good sign.*

Why? You ask.

Because attorneys only get paid *when* and *if* they win your claim. And we know a claim can take years to be decided sometimes. The attorney knows he is going to invest hours and hours working on your case, so if the attorney takes it on, you have a good idea it has promise.

To sum it up, if *you* don't win and don't get benefits, the attorney gets *nothing*.

So, we all want to make sure that neither the attorney or the claimant is wasting their time. Everybody wins in that situation because no one, including the claimant, wants to spend years pursuing a losing case.

Get proper representation and *get it right the first time!*

Now, why am I focusing so much on the attorney and not the claimant?

Because the opinion of an experienced attorney will tell you if you have a chance at winning and what needs to be done to ensure you have a higher chance at winning.

If an attorney tells you that you are wasting your time filing now, it's usually a good indication that you should wait to file and you should work on what the attorney suggested you do to get your case ready to file (*attorneys don't always get it right, but usually they do on case selection*)

You are also thinking: *"If my case is a winning case, why do I need an attorney?"*

Because a disability claim is not just filing and *hoping for the best*. There is a lot of work involved.

If you get denied, which happens more often than not, no matter how good your case, there is an appeal process which is quite involved; more evidence to be submitted, forms that need to be completed *properly*. And if your case is set for a hearing, you will have a lot of ongoing participation and assistance with preparation that your attorney will need from you.

It's not just telling your story to the judge and it's all good. There is so much more to be done.

The whole point of this section is this:

We all want to know the future if our claim is a winner. Unfortunately, no one can predict the future even an attorney. But there are many things in your case that tells an experienced attorney what your chances are even if there is more work to be done.

Now that we covered why an attorney wants a good case, let's learn what a good case looks like from the attorney's point of view.

What is the attorney (and the "decision maker") looking for in a good case?

Hint: Good quality medical records.

But, what does that mean?

Good quality medical records tell us very clearly that there is something amiss with your condition. And I'm not talking about diagnosis only. I am talking about good descriptions in the records and about details in the records that make that particular record useful in supporting your claim for disability.

In my post **Is it Time to Get Rid of Dr. X?**, I talk about certain things that doctors can do that can really mess up your medical records (find this article at the end of the chapter – page 71 – Reading Assignment Tactic 3). But the important thing to concentrate on when looking at a medical record is identifying certain basic information that will have significance to your particular medical condition.

Medical Records Reading 101

Medical records are comprised of several parts that are relevant for a disability claim.

You should know that medical records vary from doctor to doctor in style and wording since there are a number of medical note software programs on the market now and in use by doctors' offices, and those software-programs are not usually standardized.

But most of these programs at least contain the time-tested mechanism called "**S.O.A.P**" notes: **S**ubjective, **O**bjective, **A**ssessment and **P**lan. This is basically the *"skeleton"* of a medical record.

We will be going over what you are likely to see in your treatment records, and what those things mean.

To get the most out of this lesson, see if you have an old medical record around the house to go over as we talk about each item that you'll usually see on a medical record. It will make more sense for you if you can link the lesson with an actual record.

So here it goes:

1. Reason for the medical visit, ...*i.e.*, your "medical complaints"

Sometimes you see an abbreviation like **"c/o"** or something similar). This record-acronym refers to **you** telling your doctor *why* you are there for that particular visit.

Example:

Reason for Appointment

1. Migraine Headaches

These notes tend to be at the top of your medical record and they are mostly short notes just like in the image above.

This section also typically contains such references as *"dizziness"*, *"fatigue"*, *"heart palpitations"*, etc., ...*i.e.*, the things being treated on that medical visit.

2. History of Current Illness or "Subjective" (...your *"Subjective"* Complaints – the "S" in S.O.A.P)

This is usually found below item 1 (*that we covered directly above*) and this part of the record usually contains information that **you** relayed to your doctor. So, when your doctor asks you how you are feeling at the beginning of your appointment, this section is where he/she will put **your** answers.

Example:

Reason for Appointment

1. Migraine Headaches

History of Present Illness

<u>New/Follow-up Patient Consult</u>:

Patient is a ███████ lady was presenting for chronic migraines. She has had migraines for most of her Life and in the last few years they have worsened. She is on ███ patient has been on multiple medications Including ███████ currently and has tried ██████████ and other prophylactic medication which She does not remember. She has seen a few neurologist. Patient is also tried over the counter pain medications don't help. ███ is only one which helps but she cannot get more than a month which limits her. She has never been offered ████. She does report at least ███ headache which as migraine-like. There is some headaches which do not have migraine-type component but majority of the headaches, throbbing nausea photophobia phonophobia. She has about ■ or ■ headache free days during a month.

3. Review of Systems (still part of the "S" part of SOAP)

This is usually the next thing you will see in most medical records. It is a bit like an assessment list, but from **your** point of view. It's a little different than the *'historical'* part of the record because it gets a little more technical.

Notice that in this "Review of Systems" sections, the doctor discusses *all parts of your body*, not just the chief complaint you came to the doctor for that day.

This is important, for example, if you have a Migraine or some other medical condition but are also having intestinal issues or some other unusual symptoms. When the doctor sees that, he/she knows they might need to *"tweak"* your medications, because you may be having serious side effects.

Example:

Review of Systems

Hematology/Lymphatic:
Easy Bleeding denies. Easy bruising denies. Recurrent infections denies.
General:
Fatigue **admits**, Fever denies. Weight gain denies. Weight loss denies.
Ophtahmologic:
Vision loss denies. Blurred vision **admits**. Eye Pain denies. Double vision denies.
ENT:
Jaw pain denies. Jaw popping/clicking denies. Hearing loss denies. Ear pain denies. Ringing in the ears denies. Snoring denies.
Respiratory:
Cough denies. Wheezing denies.
Cardiovascular:
Lightheadedness **admits**. Passing out **admits**. Chest pain/pressure denies. Cheat pain denies. Irregular heartbeat denies. Palpitations denies.
Gastrointestinal:
Abdominal pain denies. Constipation denies. Diarrhea denies. Nausea **admits**. Vomiting **admits**.
Genitourinary:
Kidney stones denies. Urinary retention or urgency denies. Urinary incontinence denies.
Musculoskeletal:
Neck pain **admits**. Mid or lower back pain denies. Sore muscles **admits**. Cramps denies.
Skin:
Hair loss denies. New rashes denies. Skin ulcerations denies. Hives denies.
Neurology:
Balance difficulty denies. Coordination denies. Dizziness denies. Headaches denies. Memory loss denies. Seizures denies. Tingling/numbness denies. Tremor denies.
Psychiatric:
Panic attacks denies. Depression **admits**. Visual or auditory hallucinations denies. Anxiety **admits**.

4. "Objective", or "General Examination", or "Physical Examination" (the "O" in SOAP)

This is where the gold is!

This, my friends, is where the attorney will focus on with laser precision (*I can just hear the laser sounds: peew, peew, peew!*)

This is what makes or breaks a case!

Sure, you need to tell the doctor how you feel (*"Subjective"* and/or *'Review of Systems'*) but the observations by your doctor on the *"Objective/Physical Exam"* part of the records tells the *"decision maker"* or the attorney, **what the doctor** is actually seeing when he examines you.

This part is an assessment but from the **doctor's point of view**. It tells us how bad things are from the *"outside"* or from *someone else's* point of view.

For example: Imagine that you have a bad back. When the doctor examines you he/she will conduct an examination or consult where they test the movements of your back, legs, and arms (*flexion, extension*) to see how your back is limiting your movements.

And in this examination, perhaps you may be able to stretch your leg but if you do that you may see that the leg starts shaking quite a bit. Your doctor may ask you to raise your arms, but you can't lift them higher than your shoulders. He can also ask you to walk with one foot in front of the other and you may lose your balance right there. If he does a pin prick test on your feet and you can't feel them, there may be neurological deficits there.

If these are the deficits the examination reveals in your case, then these are the things we hope your doctor is writing in the *Observations/Physical Examination* part of your records. The point is, whatever your examination results, we would hope that the doctor is duly recording them.

The *"Objective" part* of the records is important because you can be very sick, yet a judge or even an attorney might only believe you if a *"third party"*, namely your doctor, is reporting those symptoms he/she sees during the examination.

That's because your doctor's credibility is seen under the social security regulations and practice as *much higher* than your credibility. In other words, the judge is obligated to follow the medical evidence of record, but he/she is not supposed to find in your favor based only upon *your* testimony.

I'm not saying the judge thinks you are lying, but there are some people (those claimants who are *"faking it"*) who will lie or *exaggerate* symptoms just to get benefits. Yet your testimony, though important, will not carry as much *"weight"* as your doctor(s)' opinions. And that is why you may hear how hard it is to win a claim for *"invisible"* conditions (*impairments that are pain related but do not show up on imaging studies, for example*).

I like to use the example of a stereo to describe how hard it is to prove pain in *"invisible cases"*:

Imagine you are listening to some music. Your favorite tune comes on, you crank the volume button a little higher to hear a little better. The sense of hearing is clear: You can tell when the music is louder.

Unfortunately, other than seeing that you don't look that well that day, no one can tell how *"loud"* your pain is inside your body. Not *"looking well"* can happen to anyone, even people who are not disabled. Yet the pain is there and is *"pretty loud"* to you.

That's why only the "big picture" will tell us how serious your conditions are.

Here's how the "Objective" part of the record looks when it's an "invisible" impairment, such as Migraines:

Examination
General Examination:
   GENERAL APPEARANCE: in no acute distress, well developed, well nourished, well Hydrated. HEAD: normocephalic, atraumatic. EYES: pupils equal, round, reactive to light and Accommodation. EARS: normal. NOSE: nares patent, no lesions, septum intact. ORAL CAVITY: Mucosa moist. THROAT: clear. NECK/THRYOID: neck supple, full range of motion, no cervical lymphadenopathy. SKIN: no suspicious lesions, warm and dry. HEART: no murmurs, regular rate and rhythm, nontender, nondistended. EXTREMITIES: no clubbing, cyanosis, or edema.
Neurological Exam:
   CORTICAL FUNCTIONS: normal. SPEECH: normal. CRANIAL NERVES: no afferent pupil defect. No ptosis or nystagmus, Pinkprick, light touch intact in all three divisions, I – Not Tested., II – Pupils 4mms reacting briskly to 2 mms, III, IV, VI – EOM were full with normal pursuit and saccade V – Motor V intact, VII – No asymmetry or weakness, VIII – Actuity intact to finger rub bilaterally, IX, X – Palate rose in the midile., XI – Sternocleidomastoid, trapezius strength intact., XII – Tongue protruded midline w/o atrophy or fasciculations. MOTOR STRENGTH: no cogwheeling, no drift. SENSORY: normal bilateral lower extremities. REFLEXES: bilaterally symmetrical, Babinski negative. PLANTARS: downgoing
bilaterally. CEREBELLAR SIGNS: absent. TREMORS: absent. TREMORS absent. COORDINATION: finger-to-nose and rapid alternating movements were intact, no ataxia. GAIT AND STATION: within normal limits, Romberg was negative.

Notice that there's nothing spectacular about this note?

The person is not in distress, most things are listed as normal, or intact. But we know the person is in bad shape. I also see this *'understated'* description quite a bit in records for heart disease cases. The records show the person is *"normal"*, but in truth this person is a *"ticking time bomb"*.

So, what do we do in a situation like this?

Basically, the attorney will take a look at the *overall picture* of the medical reports (*not just the objective part*) and also the treatment plan. But in an invisible condition scenario, what's usually the *"gold"* portion of the consult record (*objective*) is no more valuable than tin. Thus, the goal at this juncture of examining the records for the 'invisible condition' is to get the "big picture" rather than just focusing on the *"juicy"* stuff we attorneys usually look for in the "Objective" part of the records.

Now let's talk about the next part of the medical records that are crucial to the big picture for both the *'invisible'* condition cases and for *'regular'* condition cases:

5. Assessment/or Findings (the "A" in SOAP)

This is the *"diagnosis"* part of the records. It tells us not only your general diagnosis but also the doctor's ideas about what's going on with you.

For example, you are in the doctor's office for a Migraine and in your subjective complaint you told him that your eyes hurt a lot when you are outside. He will probably conclude you have a secondary diagnosis that is associated with your Migraine: Photophobia.

The same goes for Diabetes; for example, the doctor can tell you have diabetes, but now you are also complaining that your feet are numb and/or that you feel pins and needles in your feet: the secondary diagnosis is likely Diabetic Neuropathy.

So, in this part of the record, your doctor will list everything that he/she is seeing, including the connection between primary and secondary conditions: A Migraine with photophobia, Diabetes with neuropathy. *See how that works?*

Now one very important thing to know (*and you heard me say this before*):

Diagnosis alone will not win cases!

Your records *must* show symptoms and limitations that clearly prevent you from working. People have heart attacks and go back to work. People have cancer and go back to work.

The question is: *"What symptoms, despite all treatment, prevent you from working?"*

Let me give you an example:

In the medical records, your doctor says you have uncontrolled diabetes, despite insulin. You also have numbness on your feet, morbid obesity and swelling on your legs.

How do these particular symptoms prevent you from working?

A claimant with uncontrolled diabetes may experience severe fatigue, not only because of the insulin deficiency and blood sugar variations, but also because of obesity.

The person is so fatigued that she can't exercise or even go up some steps. Because the claimant can't exercise, she will continue to have issues with diabetes. It's a vicious circle the person can't get out of.

In addition to the above symptoms, the person in this scenario has numbness on the feet which will probably prevent her from taking a job that requires a lot of standing.

She will also not be able to sustain a *"sitting"* job, because if she sits for too long her legs will swell a lot and she will be required to elevate the legs. Have you ever tried to work on a computer and sitting at a desk with your legs elevated? *You can't!*

In this example, it is clear that the symptoms and limitations shown in the records prevent this person from working.

Which brings us to the other important part of the records:

Plan/Treatment/or "Treatment Plan" (the "P" in SOAP): This is where the doctor will describe the treatment available for your diagnosis, in general or for that visit. He/she can prescribe medications, order films (*MRIs, CTs*), labs, and other testing and/or referrals to other doctors.

The reason attorneys pay attention to this part of the record is because it tells us a bit more about the severity of the impairment. For example, if you have the sniffles and the doctor prescribes over-the-counter-medications, there is nothing *'exciting'* in that record. But if your doctor is recommending surgery and telling you that it's a 50-50% chance on the outcome, that is significant for your claim...*lights go off, alarms sound!*

Of course, people have surgery and go back to work all the time, but the kind of surgery being done and the follow-up visits after the surgery will tell us if you have not made meaningful improvements despite medical treatment. If you have not, then that is also quite significant for your claim.

Going back to the 'Migraine example' (*where the Objective stuff was less than compelling from a disability standpoint*), if we take a look at the *"Plan"* section of the record and it indicates injections or some other more *'radical'* treatment, then this *"Plan"* part of the S.O.A.P notes helps make up for the *less-than-wonderful "Objective"* segment. So, in that example, despite the *'Objective'* un-clarity and the *'normal'* examination, there is something else in the records that helps establish that things are *not* normal for you.

Other minor parts of the records:

As referenced above, medical records can vary from doctor to doctor because of the different medical software that different doctors use.

Even so, there are other parts of most doctors' medical records that may not be "**gold**" (*from a disability standpoint*), but still at least contain some "**silver**" or maybe "**bronze**" level information: ...and put some of those together, and maybe you turn your evidentiary picture back into "**gold**".

These bronze/silver categories include:

1. **Vitals** – height, weight, blood pressure (obesity, high blood pressure in cardiac cases, for example)

2. **Family History** – if relatives or parents had other medical conditions that could explain what you have right now. ...e.g., Genetic conditions like MS or Parkinson's.

3. **Social History** – Tobacco, alcohol, and drug abuse. If your medical condition was started by and/or was exacerbated by of one of these "vices": e.g., for conditions such as IBS, Pancreatitis and COPD, etc., 'vices' such as tobacco use can actually hurt your case if you are still doing them. Get help, now!

4. **List of Medications** – You may be taking vitamins, which is not that exciting for your claim evidence; on the other hand, if you are taking Morphine, that's something from the record to take note of.

The list is enormous, but these are some common things you might find in many medical records.

Homework

If you read this chapter with a copy of one of your records by your side, you are well on your way to understanding what to look for in your medical records.

What I want you to do for today's Tactic exercise is:

1. Make a separate pile of medical records for each of the doctors that you have.

   This part of the Tactics exercise may take you a few days more if you do not have a copy of your records. Try to get the last year or two of medical records from *each* doctor you have (*unless you haven't seen the doctor for that long*).

2. Organize those records by date, starting from the oldest to the most recent.

   And once you have organized them by date, start going over each of them with what we have covered in this section.

   Take notes on a separate piece of paper (*not on our Checklist, yet*) of everything you see in your records that we have identified in this segment as important.

   Do you see a pattern? Does your doctor repeat the same descriptions every time you go in? Is there anything serious he is listing in the Objective part of the exam or the treatment? How about the history or those minor areas like vitals?

3. Gathering information from those medical records, now you can write on your Checklist in the Treatment page (page 3): Include the information requested: *Doctor name, what he/she treats you for, Treatments Done, Treatment Dates, Date of your Last Consult, Records that you've ordered, and the Record that you received.*

   This list will not only give you an idea of the timeline of your treatment, but it will also tell us how much treatment you received and if there are *"gaps"* in your treatment.

   For example, say it has been a year since you last saw your spinal surgeon. From the standpoint of proving your disability claim, this is not good because it shows a *"gap"* of months without treatment, and little to no treatment usually is taken to mean that your impairment is *"not that bad"* from the viewpoint of the Social Security Administration.

4. Please read my article on **Cost Effective Ways to Get Your Medical Records** if you need to order them before working on this assignment (access the article at the end of this chapter – page 79 – Reading Assignment Tactic 3).

   Trust me you will want to learn those tricks for ordering records throughout the pendency of your disability claim. And in that post, I also talk a little more about the *"good quality"* medical records we discussed earlier in this book. In fact, even if you have all your records on hand, you will still want to read that post just to reinforce today's tactics.

One final thought for Today's Tactics:

This Checklist you are working on *can* and *should* be used at all stages of the claim process.

If you get denied, you should continue with medical treatment, of course. But if you also continue organizing your records and listing them on the Checklist, you will never lose sight of the direction and thoroughness of your treatment, and whether you have "*gaps*" in treatment, and whether you need to consult with more or different types of doctors, or schedule more medical consults to ensure your case is well documented.

Do you want to see a disability attorney crying tears of joy? Bring him/her your records organized in the way we have learned in this challenge. I would be sooo happy if all my clients did that.

And there is another time when that Checklist will come in handy: When it is time to fill out forms from Social Security and they ask a whole bunch of questions. Many can be answered by what you've prepared on that list!

Didn't I tell you it would all come together in the end?

OK! I know I tortured you enough. But I cannot emphasize enough how important this is and how far ahead you will be compared to others who are filing their claim without knowing this information or going through this preparatory process.

Take your time and get some rest in between tasks. I know it's a lot, but you are doing great!

Reading Assignment Tactic 3

A. Is It Time to Get Rid of Doctor X to Win Social Security?

A doctor can make or break a disability claim. Without *"good quality"* medical records you simply cannot win your disability claim.

Now, let's talk about an issue I come across very frequently and it is really important.

I'm talking about claimants who have been treating with the same doctor for many years and how that can translate into *"poor quality"* medical records.

Introducing "Dr. X"

You love Dr. X. He's been treating you for ten, fifteen, twenty years. He knows you. He knows all about your medical impairments over the years. Now you need to file for disability and you think: *"Dr. X knows everything about me. I'm all set!"*

Unfortunately, it's not always the case.

In fact, in my experience, *the longer a doctor has been treating a patient the more complacent he/she will be about the treatment.*

There are a few ways to interpret the statement above:

1. Dr. X knows your medical file so much that he doesn't even bother writing complete notes like most doctors do;

2. Dr. X is very *set in his ways* and will not try a new treatment because has been around a while and thinks he knows everything;

3. Dr. X and you have a silent agreement: He doesn't have to go out of his way to treat you and you don't ask too many questions. You just do what he says.

So, let's break these 3 statements down:

Dr. X knows you for years and years, but his medical notes are very sparse.

Why would Dr. X not write a lot of notes on your medical file?

Simple: If he has been treating you for many years he knows every detail about you. *He remembers you and all the details of your treatment.*

You see, most medical notes are not necessarily for the patient or anyone else to see (*with a few exceptions*). These notes are mostly used by the doctor to *remember* a particular patient's treatment and diagnosis.

Can you imagine a doctor remembering information from every single patient he has? That would be nearly impossible. That's why medical notes exist.

Now put yourself in his position. If you remember someone and their story do you really have to write it down?

No. Because you remember.

And that's when problems can develop:

When a doctor knows so much about you and remembers every detail about your medical issues, his medical notes tend to be sparse. *Why?*

Repeat after me: *"It's because he knows me"*. He doesn't need to read his notes to remember the details of your medical issues.

When a doctor knows you, he tends to jot down *the bare minimum* and only because there may be some minor changes to medications or a new symptom you are reporting.

And this translates into *"poor quality"* medical notes for those occasions when *you* really need them, *i.e.* when filing for disability.

What exactly does "poor quality" records mean?

It simply means that no one can tell by the content of the notes what is really going on in the mind of the doctor. The notes also fail to clearly indicate that *your symptoms are severe enough to disable you.*

You may see diagnosis (which we know is not enough on its own to qualify you for disability), perhaps some information about medications, and maybe a little bit about your complaints. ...but very little about observations by the doctor and what he *really* "sees" during each consult.

Simply stated: *Your doctor may know your medical file really well based upon his memory, but a judge cannot read your doctor's mind* and whatever is not on paper essentially *does not* exist for the judge!

Your doctor may know and believe you are disabled but if he fails to write his thoughts down, then you have little to show to prove your disability precludes you from working.

Dr. X thinks he/she knows everything and will not try a different treatment

Occasionally, I come across claimants who have a doctor who simply will not try anything new.

I'm not a doctor by any means, but it is not uncommon in my practice to know that a new treatment exists and learn that a claimant's doctor never offered that treatment to his patient.

I sometimes wonder if the doctor is simply not "evolving" along with new science or is simply *"too cocky"* and thinks he/she knows everything.

In a case like that, it becomes apparent to the judge that the patient did not have all possible treatments available for his medical conditions. If so, *how does this patient know he's disabled if not all treatment options were exhausted?*

A judge is not a doctor either

But just like me, the judge sees quite a few medical records every day. He/she is also familiar with most treatments available out there for the most common impairments. If a judge sees that not all treatment options were exhausted, *he/she will be less likely to award a claim.*

There will always be a question in the judge's mind: *"what if this claimant tried this treatment and it worked?"*

The medical records from this particular doctor will reflect this doctor's *"lack of care"* (*pun intended*).

Which brings me to the next situation:

Dr. X and you have a silent agreement

Some doctors are so busy with patients that they just don't want to nor have time to go out of their way for a patient. And patients are usually so trusting of doctors that they think what a doctor says is *"gospel"*; following what they say *blindly* and without question.

This situation can be very damaging to a disability case.

A doctor who has no time for a patient is not doing any favors to that patient. And a patient who follows a doctor blindly may be missing other available treatment that could improve his/her life.

The sad part is when a claimant comes to my office and I see that the doctor didn't even offer the most basic testing. Or worse, the claimant has a medical condition that clearly requires a specialist and yet the doctor never made a referral.

I say it's sad because 1) the claimant is filing for disability without proper medical testing for a clear diagnosis, and 2) the claimant never saw a specialist who could have offered better treatment with the possibility of a cure.

And if that's what your records reflect, in a way it is *"too early"* to file the claim because not all of the potential treatments have been explored; and it is unclear if a claimant is really disabled without proper treatment.

So, is it time to get rid of Dr. X?

Maybe. Maybe not. That will depend on a lot of things.

1. Is he the only doctor treating you?

    If so, I would suggest asking for a referral to a specialist if you think your treatment reached a *plateau*.

2. Are you able to get a second opinion just to see if a *"fresh"* set of eyes can find some other treatment for your condition?

    Maybe your doctor has known you for so long that he just spends more time chatting than actually looking at your chart.

3. If you started asking questions about your treatment, would your doctor listen to you or would he just *brush it aside?*

   A lot of doctors *"raise their feathers"* if you try to dig a little deeper or when you ask why you should take a particular medication. If this is the reaction, please refer back to item 2 above.

Here's something to think about also:

   A. **What does your gut instinct tell you about your doctor?** You may like him/her, but is he/she really doing everything they can? I once had a doctor who was a sweetheart and he loved to chat. But the actual examination would last only 5 minutes compared to 25 minutes of menial conversation. It was nice having a doctor who spent time with me. *But how much of that time was really dedicated to my treatment?*

   B. **Since you know Dr. X for a long time, are you able to ask him/her to improve your medical notes?** Would he/she be willing to do so? Now, if he/she agrees then this will certainly benefit you.

   C. **If your doctor is not going to change the notes, is he/she at least willing to testify at your disability hearing?** This may help overcome his *"sparsely"* written medical records. And the doctor doesn't even have to be present at the hearing. Doctors can appear by telephone.

I know it's hard to make changes in your life, especially when it comes to finding a good doctor. But if you are looking to win your disability claim, you need to pay attention to your treatment before it's too late. Otherwise, it will all be a waste of time. We don't want that.

I want you to win!

B. Cost Effective Ways to Order Medical Records and Save Money

Medical records are a vital part of a disability case.

Whether it's Social Security or Short/Long Term Disability, you will only win your case with good quality medical records. We talked about how important they are in my post about the **15 reasons people get denied disability** (Reading Assignment Tactics 2 – page 37).

What does a "Good Quality Medical Record" mean?

Good quality medical records are notes from your doctor which describe very well what your medical conditions are. Ideally, they should also describe how your physical or mental impairments affect your ability to work.

These records should show what your *Subjective* complaints are, i.e., *how you feel*. They should also show *Objective* findings. That is, the doctor writes down what he/she sees or notices when they examine you.

There must also be an *Assessment*. This is kind of similar to objective findings, but the doctor is now describing what the medical issue is based on his *objective* findings.

Finally, the notes should show the *treatment* plan your doctor is recommending for your condition. Those treatments can include medications, injections, therapy, surgery, etc.

Now that we know what the medical records should show, it's time to talk about how to get them from your doctor.

Should an Attorney Order Your Medical Records?

A lot of attorneys don't order records for prospective clients due to cost. If every attorney ordered records just to see if a case was worth taking, that attorney would be broke in the first week of opening his doors.

Attorneys who do order records for prospective clients will certainly come back to the client with a bill eventually.

Here's a secret that you may not know:

I know it's convenient to have someone else do the *leg-work* for you and order your medical records. But if an attorney orders medical records on your behalf this **will cost you more money!**

Do you know why?

Doctors are used to getting requests from personal injury attorneys that do cases like car-crashes. And Injury attorneys usually pay *top dollar* for those records. So, some doctors charge those rates thinking that disability attorneys have to do the same thing.

If you ask for the records yourself, some doctors may even give them to you for free. *Or at least, at a very low cost.*

The secret when ordering medical records is:

Do not mention you have a lawyer! (or even that the records are for a disability claim).

And don't tell your doctor that you are looking for a lawyer. A lot of medical office managers or receptionists will balk at your request if you mention there is a lawyer involved, because they see dollar signs in exchange for the records. Some of them may even tell you that you are not entitled to your records and that only your attorney can get them.

This is not true! …but some of them will do it anyway in order to make a buck for their office on your record request.

What you *should* say instead is that you need your medical records for your own personal reasons.

That's it!

No need for too much explanation by you. Medical provider offices are usually permitted by State law to charge some minimum amount for the records, but it is usually such a small amount, they often don't even bother.

I also found that sometimes if you ask your doctor directly for a copy of your records instead of asking his receptionist you will get less resistance and/or *"up-charging"* in connection with your request.

Of course, sometimes the doctor is too busy, or his/her office has its own rules about records request. But know that if you order them yourself instead of expecting your attorney to do it, you will save a lot of money in the long run.

You may be thinking, *"Why am I hiring an attorney if he/she can't even take care of that part of the claim?"*

Well, number one, a good disability attorney knows you don't have a lot of money. So, if that attorney is any good he will do everything possible to help you *save money*. One of the ways to save a client's money is to allow the client to do some of the legwork in their case.

Second, the real work only begins *after* the records arrive at the attorney's desk, *not before*.

Third, your Social Security disability attorney is not, as a practicality permitted under Social Security regulation to easily advance the costs of your medical records like a personal injury attorney does. The way a personal injury attorney advances such costs is to charge back against the settlement funds. But in Social Security cases, the benefits distribution operates differently, and your attorney, if he/she is operating within the permissible Social Security fee regulations, has no guarantee of seeing advanced costs for things such as medical records returned if they are going to keep your costs at a minimum.

So, this is about teamwork!

Your role is to go to the doctor for treatment and get the medical records. And the attorney's role is to get those records you provided and work his/her *"magic"*.

Saving money should always be in the mind of the attorney since the claimant usually doesn't have any money and *case-costs* recompense is not assured even with an attorney-client representation agreement.

Even if your attorney does end up advancing costs in your case, most clients don't like surprises when paying back an attorney, thus you should get a clear and up-front picture of what the costs would be if the attorney must do some of the legwork for you.

And if the attorney says he doesn't charge for that service, get it in writing! I don't like surprises when I pay fees, you should not either.

To Recap:

- Medical records are notes provided by your doctor describing your medical conditions and treatment plan.
- Most attorneys will charge extra for ordering medical records on your behalf.
- If you are looking to save money in your case, *you* should order the medical records directly from your doctors. Remember, don't mention the records are for a disability claim or it will cost you more.
- Avoid requesting that the records be sent to the attorney's office even if you are the one requesting them. Some medical offices end up billing the attorney who will then have to charge you!

Tactic 4 – The Big Picture and Putting It All Together

Can You Believe How Much You've Learned So Far?

Tactic 1 – "Sign up", you opened an account with SSA and learned about PIA, AOD, and DLI.

Tactic 2 – You Learned about the difference between SSDI and SSI and also about the importance of your medical records and how to fix them to improve your chances of winning your case.

Tactic 3 – You learned how to properly read your medical records and how to spot if your records are telling the whole story about your disability. You also got a glimpse into the mind of an attorney and what we look for when we are evaluating a case for possible representation.

It's a lot! But now we will be putting all this together so that you can file your case.

Let's get to Tactic 4 first!

By now, I hope you are seeing the big picture of your particular case. Hopefully, you are using your Checklist you got in Tactic 1 and have been making notes on it each step of the way.

If you did so, you probably have the following information down:

- You know your PIA (how much you are paid per month if you win your case)
- You have your DLI (date last insured) and you know when it expires so you can figure out if you are at a disadvantage in trying to win your SSDI benefits, or negates your ability to file, leaving a filing for SSI benefits as your only potential recourse.
- You know your AOD (the date you stopped working or another date like we discussed on Tactic 1)
- You wrote down all the names and addresses of your doctors and your treatment.
- You organized all your medical records from the previous years to the present (one or two years are usually enough).
- You read your medical records and took notes about what you saw in them that support your disability.
- In Tactic 2, you read about how to fix your records and you learned from the articles that you should find the right doctors (*specialists*) to treat your most severe impairments[§].

[§] Note: this task is not necessary prior to filing your claim but starting now is a great idea as the process of fixing/building your records can take as

Hopefully, in Tactic 3, you also spotted any gaps in your medical treatment, and if such gaps are ongoing, you should strongly consider more consults with your doctor(s).

Now, let's run one through one sample filing of a disability case, from start to finish (*pre-filing to filing*), to make sure you have this down and you understand everything so far.

Filing Scenario

Claimant "M" was diagnosed with severe Post Traumatic Stress Disorder (PTSD) following a traumatic event on January 1, 2015.

"M" is 45 years old and works as a mechanic in a very busy and noisy shop. Because of the PTSD, he can't handle noises. He has a panic attack whenever he hears something fall on the ground and leaves work early *"to deal with it"*.

He sees a primary care doctor only who gives him some medications to contain the panic attacks. But the meds only *"take the edge off"*. He also went to a psychiatrist once and did a few sessions with a therapist but stopped going because *"the treatment wasn't working"* in his opinion.

"M" decided to stop working on March 15, 2015. Staying on the job was too much for him. He opened an account with SSA and found out his **PIA** is about **$1,130.00**. His **DLI** is **December 2020** and his **AOD** is **March 15, 2015**: The day he stopped working.

---

long as your entire claim process. In other words, if you get into a specialist now but you get denied after filing, you can at least have better records for the next round (the appeal).

He goes to the Social Security Office and files his case in June 2015. Four months later he receives a notice that he was denied.

Now, why do you think he was denied?

Here are my findings:

1. **He filed his case too early.** He filed only 3 months after quitting.

    We learned from our reading (*Tactic 1*) that you must prove that your condition has lasted or is expected to last 12 months or more to qualify for benefits. We also learned that the clock starts ticking when the person stopped working.

    In this scenario, even if he had the PTSD for ten years but continued working, it was still the wrong time to file because it hadn't been 12 months since he stopped working. I'm not saying you can't file your claim, but you will most likely be denied because of that *"12-month"* rule.

    Always remember you can use your original AOD whenever you file. So, even if you wait two years to file, that AOD is preserved and potentially you will have a large amount of accrued *"back-benefit"* waiting for you when you finally win (*though your back pay may only include a period of no more than a year prior to filing*).

2. **He only sees a primary doctor and not a specialist.**

    PTSD is a serious mental impairment. We are not talking about the *"sniffles"* here. A primary doctor can treat a lot

Tactic 4 – The Big Picture and Putting It All Together

of medical conditions, even some mild *depression* cases. But as competent as your primary doctor is, he/she should really be referring you to a specialist.

You read my posts about medical records as part of your assignment, and you know by now that primary doctors know a *"little bit of everything"* but specialists know *"a LOT about one thing"*: **Your severe impairment.**

Do you want someone who has *"some"* idea how to treat your specialized condition treating you? Or do you prefer someone who has been treating thousands of cases just like yours for years and *knows a lot* more about it?

I vote for years of experience any day.

So why did "M" get denied?

SSA probably thought that his PTSD was not very serious because "M" was not going to the *right* doctors to get treated. In this case, he needed a Psychiatrist for medications and probably a Psychologist for counseling too (***Please consult your own doctor for advice on proper treatment*).

3. Since "M's" medical records were from a primary doctor only, the SSA couldn't tell if he might improve if he just treated with a specialist. The records would not support disability in this situation since it is not clear from these records that "M" would not significantly improve with proper treatment.

4. Or, it is possible that if he treated with a specialist, "M" could improve enough to be able to work *"some other job"*

aside from the work he used to do, …even if he is not trained for the new job and even if it doesn't pay as much. If SSA finds a job he can do with his limitations, the case is closed, and he loses.

So, what does it mean to a case if you know you're disabled but your records don't show that?

It just means you did not meet your "burden of proof".

What does "burden of proof" mean for my disability case?

For most claimants, particularly those under 50 years old, it means that *you*, the claimant, must prove you are *permanently* disabled. It is *your* responsibility to bring *"good quality"* records that clearly show that you cannot do *any* jobs at all.

If the records are missing important facts about your symptoms and limitations, they may leave too much for interpretation, and that usually works against you.

Temporary Disability

You may be wondering: *"What if my disability is temporary but I won't be working for a long time?"*

While there is such a thing as *"closed-period"* disability benefits, winning those cases can be tricky if at some point during the case you go back to work.

Imagine that you will be going in front of a judge two years after filing and six months prior to the hearing you went back to work. While the rules allow you to file for that, the reality is that if you are working, the judge will have no incentive to pay your claim.

It's all about that *"permanently disabled"* status *thingy*!

What Should "M" Do After His Denial?

We are going to talk about that a lot more soon, but for now, you should know that "M" MUST appeal his case, even with the imperfections we found in his case.

Can you spot anything else wrong in his case that could explain his denial?

Please share your findings in the Facebook Group so others can learn too. I would love to see how many other issues my readers can find.

The other thing to remember from our reading is that during the pendency of your case (*i.e.,* after the filing) if you know you need to *"fix"* your treatment, do it during that time and keep doing so throughout the case.

You never know.

What if your medical records improved enough that you win in the next round?

The idea is that if your impairments are genuine and your functional restriction is sufficiently severe as to bring you into that class of people whom Congress intends to pay under this Title (*U.S.C. Title 24; Social Security Disability*)… you should *never give up!*

Homework for Tactic 4

We know the next Tactic is "Filing Day".

Can you believe you are this close to filing your case?

In Tactic 5, I will go over the various methods of filing, so you can select the one you prefer or the most convenient for you. But before you file your claim, there is some additional document gathering you should do.

Below, you will find some important links from the SSA website. I want you to either print or download them for today's homework and start working on them now.

Each link provides an official list of documents or information (*not just medical*) that you should have on hand when you file your case. Some of those records will not be required right away (*depending on the method of filing*). But I want you to be prepared ahead of time anyway since everything is fresh in your head.

Here Are the Links:

1. **Checklist for an online application** (www.ssa.gov/hlp/radr/10/ovw001-checklist.pdf): I want you to gather this information even if you apply using other methods that we will talk about soon.

2. **Checklist for "in-person" filing** (www.ssa.gov/disability/Documents/Checklist%20-%20Adult.pdf). You will notice that the information is pretty similar to the checklist above. No need to do duplicate work.

3. **Fact Sheet with useful information about what happens to your case "before", "during" and "after" the filing** (www.ssa.gov/disability/Documents/Factsheet-AD.pdf). This is something you want to save for your records, so you can come back to it from time to time.

Tactic 5 – Filing Day!

I know it's a little strange to be excited about filing for disability. No one wants to be in this position. But think of it this way: *It's your financial future and security at stake*. If at least there is money coming in, we don't feel so bad that everything else is *"less-than-wonderful"*. In fact, because you will have financial stability, you will be able to focus more on getting better and not as much on the overdue bills.

Sure, you will not be receiving as much as money as you used to earn, but having a source of funds is better than no income at all.

To learn a little more about financial lifestyle changes and budgeting while living on disability, please read my article about **Balancing your budget like a pro** (access the article at the end of this chapter – page 123 – Reading Assignment Tactic 5-C).

I also have another budget article from my thrifty living blog *Amigas4all.com* where I talk about **How to create and maintain a budget without starving** (access the article at the end of this Chapter – page 129 – Reading Assignment Tactic 5-D).

Money is Not the Cure

I also want you to understand that while money is important, and the disability process can be difficult, winning your case is *not* a cure for all your troubles.

The pain and limitations will continue after you win. So please, don't stress over the process and don't make it the *main focus* of your life. You have more important things to worry about, like, *getting better*, for example.

Other Thoughts Before We Start with Tactic 5

Since you were an excellent student, you wrote everything down on your nifty Checklist from Tactic 1. You downloaded or printed the *SSA checklists* and *fact-sheet* and you gathered that information in an organized paper folder.

You also gathered all your medical records and organized them from the oldest date to the most recent medical records you have.

You have prepared for this in these past few days or weeks. You asked questions in our Facebook group and you got your questions clarified. You have your document folder and your medical records folder.

You are ready!

Tactic 5 is About Choosing Your Preferred Method of Filing and 'Taking the Plunge' of Filing Your Case

You need to know your options for actually making the filing.

There are **three methods** you can use to file the claim. I'm going to list each method and explain the pros and cons, then you will be able to choose the one you think is best for you.

Here they are:

1. "In-Person" Filing

Just like it sounds, this is the where you drive over to your local Social Security 'State-Agency' office and file your claim *in person*.

To locate the nearest office in your area type on your browser **https://secure.ssa.gov/ICON/main.jsp** and enter your zip code.

What are the 'Pros' and 'Cons' of this method?

Pros: You meet with the agent who will be taking your information face to face.

This agent will ask you a bunch of questions and will request a copy of your medical records and financial information. The agent will type everything in his/her computer system and when you leave their office, your case is officially filed.

The best part is that you didn't have to type anything.

One thing that is also good about filing in person is that if you have a medical impairment that is very visible like blindness, an amputation of a limb or extremity (*leg, feet, arm*), or have a visibly crooked spine, walk with a pronounced limp, or have a severe deformity that is clearly visible, *etc.,* ….you may have an advantage with this filing method.

The agent will make notes about what he/she *"sees"* (*your deformity, etc.*) when meeting you in person. You will probably not see their observations of your condition on your receipt for the filing or on any paperwork readily available to you, but good chance what they see will be conveyed to the *"decision maker"*.

Cons: Imagine going to the Department of Motor Vehicles. ...*Yup!* Unless you live in a small town or you happen to walk into the local office at a slow time, ...it can be *that* bad.

There is also the issue of discomfort. Imagine yourself sitting for Two hours or so with your bad back in one of those hard chairs. Or if you have anxiety or agoraphobia? ...*can you imagine being around all those people?*

Oh, and the agent will also write notes about you, describing what he/she *"sees"*. Thus, if the worker taking your application does not see anything *'disabling'* in your outward appearance, such as is the case with *'internal pain'* or *'invisible impairments'*, such as Migraine or Gastro-Intestinal disorders, then that would be a factor to consider in going with one of the other filing options. It may be that the agent taking your application writes something like: *"No visible impairments"*, *"no pain behavior"*, or things of that sort.

Do they always do that? Probably not, but it's something to think about.

The decision is up to you, but *this is not my favorite method of filing*, unless the claimant has a *"visible"* impairment like we just talked about. And even then, *why suffer* standing in line?

One other consideration is that your local office may make *'appointments'*, like the Motor Vehicle Departments have started to do; but we've heard stories that those appointments do not always guarantee that there won't still be some waiting around at the Agency office.

2. Online Filing

Just like it sounds, you file your claim online. Just type on your browser **https://secure.ssa.gov/iClaim/dib** to start the process. But before you do that, please read about the pros and cons of filing online so you can make an informed decision.

Pros: If you are computer savvy and can figure out anything online, this method of filing is for you.

Even if you have to take breaks to finish the application, you can always go back to it later. The on-line filing system actually gives you a *"reentry number"* so that you can log back in when you feel like continuing with the application. This reentry number has nothing to do with the account you just opened in Tactic 1.

With this method of filing, you don't have to drive anywhere, and you don't have to see anyone. No one has to see you either (*they will see you if and when it's time for an evaluation by an SSA-retained consultative doctor, ...but not for the filing*).

If you don't have visible impairments, or otherwise are one of those people that *'just look normal'*, rather than having an appearance of *'disabled'*, then with this method, you don't have to worry about any SSA agent writing *'looks normal'* on your application.

Cons: If you have one of those *"visible"* impairments we talked about above while discussing the *"in-person"* filing method, you would not be meeting with anyone in person with this method, and hence there will not be any opportunity for an SSA agent to make *'favorable notes'* about what they see.

If you decide to do all the work of filing online through this method in one sitting, it will likely take a couple hours, or even more, depending on your pace, and provided that you have all the information required.

Of course, because you were a good reader with all our prep-work, you actually have all that information together!

Didn't I promise you would be ready?

That's the good part. The 'not-so-good' part about filing online is that you have to manually transfer all the information you gathered.

Yes, "by hand"!

So if your back hurts when you sit for too long, or you have arthritis or carpal tunnel flares up while you are typing for an extended time, it is not a *"fun"* project.

Here's another *"kicker"* with filing online: The online application can be a bit confusing. If you click on the *wrong button* you can lose all the stuff you worked on. If you click on the wrong back button you may even be kicked out of the application. At least I have heard of that happening, though admittedly the SSA seems to have made some improvements to the program. But imagine having to start again if you lost information, or even having to re-do just part of it?

And like I said before, you really have to be at least minimally computer savvy, and even if you are, you really have to go slow to make sure you don't make a mistake. Suffice it to say, some applicants will find this method easier than other applicants. Hence much like filing *'in-person'*, filing on-line *is not my favorite method of filing.*

*Please note that this book does not provide an actual *'walk-through'* of the online application. And that's because the Social Security Administration's online application will not show the entire form if the user is not filing an *actual* claim. You may have already seen this limitation with other online *'how-to'* videos for filing.

Which brings us to my favorite method of filing: **By phone!**

3. Filing by Phone

Did I mention that this is my favorite method of filing? Here's why:

Because unlike the *"in-person"* filing, you don't have to drive anywhere, and unlike the *"online"* method, you don't have to type anything!

How easy and nice is that?!

To file by phone just call this number: **1-800-772-1213** (TTY **1-800-325-0778**). And if you are not confident with your English, they will even arrange for a translator.

Pros: Imagine being able to file your claim in the comfort of your couch, bed or recliner. You could even do this lying down! And if you have arthritis and holding the phone is too much you can also use the speaker for a *"hands-free"* filing.

Cons: Well, the SSA Agent won't see you and make notes about your *"visible"* impairments.

And I guess maybe some folks don't like this part: ...*i.e.*, the SSA will take your application in two parts:

First, they take some introductory information when you call in and start the application; and then the more involved phone-interview occurs about a week or so later; during your first phone contact with them, they will arrange a future time and date that they need you to be available by phone. But they will tell you what information you will need to have ready for this second phone session. Plus, the date that you first called in to start the phone-application will be considered your *'filing-date'* for purpose of awarded back-pay.

Do you see why this is my favorite method?

Something to be aware of with this method: you may find the SSA phone representative that you are trying to lodge your claim with is encouraging you, sometimes not so subtly, to file by computer. I think that is so that *you* would be doing the work, and not them.

Insist that he/she takes the application by phone!

Hiring an Attorney to File Your Claim

While most larger firms will file a case for you (*you will see below why it isn't always a good thing*), probably most attorneys will not file a case for you.

As you learned from this publication, a lot of the information you were gathering is readily available to you, and you can certainly forward that information over to SSA directly. There is no need for a middleman (*i.e.,* an attorney).

...and you may be thinking why hire an attorney if he won't even file my case?

If an attorney were to file your case, you would still have to gather that same information for him. All of it. *So why add another person in the mix?*

Plus, there are many advantages in filing directly with SSA. One of those is if there is a situation where you only qualify for SSI. Only the SSA can tell you if you qualify for SSI at the time of filing. As much information as you can give to an attorney, the attorney will still not have the complete picture that you would impart by directly doing the application yourself. My personal belief is that running your application through a conduit, such as an attorney's office, will likely result in lost information.

There is also the possibility, *and it does happen*, that you may win your case right after the filing and this can mean two things:

1. **If you did not hire an attorney, you won't have to pay attorney's fees to anyone.** Depending on when you filed your claim, you may have a good amount of "back-benefit" accumulated. If you file your claim and you win in the first round, all that accumulated money goes to you. *All of it!*

2. **If you did hire an attorney to file your claim and you win in the first round.** Imagine that you hire an attorney and all the attorney did was filling out the online form and helping you fill out two or three other forms, and then after 4 months or so, the SSA awards your case.

...because you have an accumulated back benefit, the attorney will get 25% of your back-benefits (or $6,000 whichever is less, as of this print). So, for Four months of work and some information gathering you attorney may get up to $6,000!

Why not wait for the decision on the first round to see if you win? Then the money goes all to you.

I'm not saying that you shouldn't hire an attorney from the beginning. *You sure can and ideally you should.* Just know that you risk paying a lot of money for just a few months of attorney work.

There is also another scenario: You hire an attorney and you win early, but there is *no* accumulated back-benefit. While you will receive your *"future"* benefits, the attorney who did all that work gets nothing (even if it's 4 months of work). *Nothing!*

That's why a lot of attorneys will not take cases until the *"first denial"*. Remember that as much as we want to help, we all have to pay our bills.

One note about attorney's fees:

Under the Social Security Disability regulations, attorneys are essentially *not allowed* to charge you upfront for a *'consultation'* to see if they will take your Social Security case.

They are also not allowed to take money from you as *'earned'* money (*from an accounting standpoint*) *ahead of time* ...they would have to hold such funds in escrow pending a lengthy approval process, which most attorneys do not want to get into.

So typically when an attorney begins representation of your case, you will on the one hand be required to sign a contingent fee agreement (*contract*) and some representation forms, but on the other hand will usually not have to pay anything other than costs (*copies, faxes, ordering records, etc.*).

Only when there is an award, will the attorney be allowed to charge for his fees, and even then, SSA has a system that pays the attorney directly out of a percentage of the back-money going to you, and the attorney would have to collect from you directly any case costs incurred (*again, such as for photocopies and postage that their office spent on behalf of your case*); that is, if the attorney doesn't just waive those costs.

What all of that basically means: If you win, you get a check for the U.S. Treasury for **75%** of the accumulated back-benefit and the attorney gets (*also direct from the U.S. Treasury*) **25%**, or $6000 (*as of this publication*). And this means that you do not have to write a check to anyone. (*There are some variations on this basic fee model if your case has to have more than one hearing and/or proceeds to Federal District Court for a higher-level appeal, but this topic is not for this publication*).

Why am I talking about attorneys again?

1. Unless you win the first round, you *will* and *should* get an attorney in your jurisdiction to appeal your case.

2. You want to know how attorneys get paid because a lot of people don't know *they don't have to pay for an attorney ahead of time*. They fail to take advantage of their ability to have an attorney simply because they think they have to come up with attorney's fees upfront when they can barely feed themselves.

Remember on Tactics 3, when we talked about how attorneys only get paid *when and if* they win your case?

Why not take advantage of this? If you get denied, **call an attorney asap!**

Just a few more things that you should know going forward:

1. Depending on the jurisdiction you are in, your claim may take several months to be decided *I know for a fact it's been taking about 4-6 months for the SSA's first 'yay' or 'nay' following (the initial application) in Arizona, where I'm from.*

2. If you get a denial letter, you have **60 days** to appeal that decision. I wrote a couple of articles about the **Denial letter** and one about **What to do when you get denied** which should help you get ready for the next step (access the articles at the end of this chapter – pages 111 and 118 respectively – Readings Assignments Tactic 5 A. and B.).

   Take some time to read them after you are done filing and are awaiting SSA's initial decision.

3. After your claim filing, the SSA will send you some forms to complete.

   Typically, those forms are seeking information about your work history, your functional capacity (*ability to do activities and what they are*) and updates on medical treatment (*you will shine on this last one since you now know from these materials to update your claim Checklist even while you wait for the SSA's decision).*

Keep an eye out for my *soon-to-be-released* book about completing your disability forms, and other tips about the disability claim process on my blog Realtactics4disabilityclaims.com. But I want you to start now by reading my article on how to properly complete your disability forms at **http://realtactics4disabilityclaims.com/properly-complete-disability-claim-forms/.**

For now, just be sure to include in your forms: *"time limitations"* (*how long you take to complete your activities - dishes, laundry*), and be sure to explain *"how difficult it is"* for you to do all of those daily activities that you disclose on the form.

Pfeew! I. AM. SO. PROUD. OF. YOU!

You are ready to make that call!

Or go online.

Or get in line at the *"MVD"*.

Go ahead! You are ready to file!

Don't be shy. You can do this!

Final Thoughts on the 5 Tactics

If you have any general questions about the filing process, feel free to ask in the Facebook Group for this book at **facebook.com/groups/realtactics4filingyourdisabilityclaim/**.

Important: If your question gets into too much detail about the merits of your case, you may need to consult an attorney in your jurisdiction. But I will let you know if this is the case.

One important thing, when you finally hire an attorney:

You will know a heck of a lot more than someone who has not read this material and/or other materials from my various blogs, and that can help you coordinate your case with your attorney and help you know what to ask your attorney and/or maybe remind your attorney about.

Remember: your attorney assumed the liability for your case, and I am not your attorney and have not assumed any liability for your case. Therefore, be sure to follow *his/her directions* as well as you can, and hopefully they are experienced and know what they are doing and have some *nice tricks* up their sleeves too.

Attorneys have different opinions on how their cases should be managed and other strategies and I would not want to step on anyone's toes.

You can read my blog posts to learn something about Social Security, and certainly you can always ask your attorney if any of the posts are relevant to your case, but I cannot answer questions directly specific to your claim, particularly if you are represented by an attorney. But even if you are not represented by an attorney, I am still not permitted (*by 'attorney rules'*) to give any more than the general type of information you are seeing in this book, as detailed as all of this has been.

If you have a lawyer, stick to his/her advice. Only they will or can know the particulars of your case

But if you used the materials and you get an early win on your case, would you please share it with the group or me? I would love to know what parts of this book you found helpful and utilized in your claim process.

I greatly appreciate your feedback on this topic and for this book, particularly if you believe others could benefit from its tactics and content; I thank you very kindly for your positive online reviews.

Thank you again for joining me and I wish great success in your claim!

Until next time,

Reading Assignment Tactic 5

(Optional Assignment Post Filing)

A. The Social Security Denial Letter: A 'canned' letter?

You applied for disability and you finally received a letter from Social Security after waiting the three-to-six months to hear from them. But the news is not as good as you expected:

It's a denial letter, that says in so many words that *'even though you have some impairments and those cause you discomfort, after "careful" consideration, we don't believe you meet the definition of disability'*. …words to that effect.

To add insult to injury they add that: either *'you can still work on your last occupation despite your impairments, or in the alternative, 'you should be able to do some other type of work'*.

Believe me, I have seen worse letters!

On one occasion, we looked at a letter on behalf of a client that listed out a ridiculously long list of very severe impairments followed by the *canned* statement that he could do other work, *etc*. The irony was almost comical to anyone not in the position of that claimant. It may as well have said, *'even though you are nearly lying in a coffin, we feel you should be able to work!'*

I have seen my share of unwarranted denial letters but that one *took the cake*. If not for privacy reasons we could have framed it.

The good news is that in the end, the client won.

You think: *"How can Social Security think I can work with all these impairments?" "How can they deny me when I sent a letter from my doctor saying I can't work?"*

First of all: Breathe!!!

Second: …Don't take this letter personally!

I'm going to tell you a secret and it's a valuable one:

Those SSA denial letters are more or less *"canned"* letters. But those letters also serve a purpose: to weed out the *"bad apples"* that apply and don't deserve benefits.

What?! **You say:** *"I paid into the system all these years and this is what I get, a canned letter?!!!"*

Well, *It's sort of a canned letter.* 75% of the language does come from a base computer *"macro"* letter that is used to produce the *final letter*. Then there are paragraphs they can use to *"customize"* it to your situation. ...*i.e.*, common statements used over and over again by the SSA with a small portion changed to list out the impairments of the particular claimant. They add your medical conditions and your name and voilà: *a nifty denial letter is ready*.

Ready to cause anxiety and frustration to the reader. Ready to cause you to doubt your own knowledge of your medical impairments and the functional restrictions you know you have.

Self-doubt sets in and Social Security is counting on that. Maybe they are counting on that, or equally likely, are just too large and/or understaffed of an organization to really care. Or they see themselves as protecting a limited and/or diminishing fund with which to pay people as the population ages, and they are doing the best they can.

Regardless, it is likely Social Security hopes with their denial of your claim that you will conclude that you can actually do some other new and/or different type of full-time competitive work, and sometimes they are right (*more on that below*). But when they are not right, it is no great mental leap to see that SSA hopes that those folks to whom a judge would eventually give a win, will be discouraged by the denial and *just give up* because the process is too lengthy and confusing.

On the one hand, denying claims is one way for Social Security to save money. On the other hand, imagine if SSA paid benefits to everyone who asked? They would be substantially broke and pretty quickly.

In a sense they already are because they have projected *end-dates* at which the fund will exhaust; yet such calculations are in another sense political, as they are malleably subject to further legislative action; the funding-status of a major agency such as SSA in some ways operates via a *'financial fiction'*, via the shifting and borrowing of assets from one federal agency to another, *etc*...but those are topic for another time.

So *why am I telling you this?* ...I'm telling you this to make you feel better!

What?! You ask: *"Is she out of her mind?!!!! How is this going to make me feel better?"*

I will tell you why, but first: back to breathing! ....and I said not to take the canned denial letter personally, *remember*?

The first thing you should know is that even if it's a denial letter, people still go on to win disability every day. *Everyday!*

Even better: I can tell you that a high percentage of people who eventually won disability benefits received these denial letters. Sometimes more than once! (*This varies from jurisdiction-check your own State, please!*).

The other thing is that Social Security does this to weed out those who are not really disabled and that either want to *"mooch"* from the system or those who are honest people but just have no clue how the system works, and simply do not know who Congress intends to pay under SSDI and whom they do not.

I will give you one example: Let's say someone worked as a truck driver. That's pretty heavy-duty work, *right?* ...Going up and down the ladder. Sometimes unloading cargo, tying ropes around the cargo loads, a lot of crouching under the truck, opening heavy doors, etc.

Now let's say this driver has a knee problem and a bad back.

This driver decides to file for disability because he says he can't work as a truck driver anymore. He applies and gets a denial.

The denial says he can do something else.

That truck-driving claimant may not have fully considered that in reality (and also by SSDI assessment), even though he cannot do truck driving anymore, he *can* actually do something else. Something a little easier. Maybe a desk job. Maybe he can supervise other drivers. It doesn't mean he wanted to take advantage of the system, but he thought his career (*truck driving*) was over and that's all he knew. Why is this claimant not thinking along these lines? ...quite likely because he is not trained for and/or would not be hired to do other types of work

As we've covered in earlier chapters, most folks don't know that the standard in Social Security is that to win disability you *must prove that* you cannot do *any jobs*.

None, period. And the government need only make a showing that in theory you have the exertional capacity to do some other line of work. Under the regulations, it is not SSA's legal burden to demonstrate that some new employer is ever actually going to hire you.

So, this claimant may not be able to do truck-driving anymore but if he/she truly can do something else Social Security will deny that claim, and such a denial would not be improper under the existing regulations. And if the available evidence from your doctors does not foreclose the possibility of alternative lines of work, then the reality of your situation will likely not save your claim from the regulatory limitations of the system.

Now, if your impairments truly *do* prevent you from working on a very long-term and/or permanent basis, then, you really should appeal the denial, ...i.e., do not feel intimidated by the *'canned'* denial letter or even in the current shortfalls in your medical evidence; you appeal and then work on improving your medical and functional evidence:

Consider that denial as part of *'the game'*!

That's right!

That denial is an *assurance* that there is more to fight for. That denial weeds out the ones who perhaps can sustain some alternative work and helps assure that only those who really deserve it will *win* in the end.

You also should know that the vast majority of my winning clients received at least one denial letter!

Did they give up? *No!*

Isn't it a relief knowing that you are not crazy in your impressions of how this process can make a claimant feel? And, isn't it a relief that despite getting bad news you know there may well be a *light at the end of the tunnel*?

Don't give up just because of that denial letter!

A wise salesman once said: *'a sale begins when client says no'*. Use that same wisdom in your case:

You keep moving forward. Life does not stop. If you give up, in a year or two you will regret not having continued with the process. Then you have to start all over and you may not qualify by then (*Remember the "DLI" limitations?*).

To Recap:

If you receive a denial letter from Social Security: *Don't hyperventilate! Don't give up!*

Appeal that denial! If you got denied you have a few options: you can appeal it online, you can call an attorney to see if he/she can take your case and appeal for you *or* contact your local Social Security office to appeal.

You have 60 days to file that appeal!

B. Why You Should Immediately Appeal Your Social Security Disability Denial

A large percentage of cases are denied on the first attempt.

What goes on in the underbellies of the Social Security State Agency offices across the nation is a mystery to most of us, including most attorneys.

Why so many early and simplistic denials?

One reason is likely because the *lower level* decision makers are simply not qualified to make that decision. In other words, the State Agency employee who denied your claim may simply be thinking that the claim needs review by a judge for *credibility* assessment or similarly less-tangible factors, such as *pain levels*, and/or *expert witness* vocational testimony at the hearing; but the SSA agent is not going to go into all that with the denial letter.

For one thing, such a comprehensive explanation would be lengthy and protracted and probably confusingly legalistic. And it may also be that not all of the agents at the Stage Agency offices would be able to cogently express those subtleties or are simply too overworked to do so.

There are reported situations where new hiring and training cannot keep up with attrition of qualified personnel at many of these offices, in part because of hiring freezes spanning several decades. Politically, not every governing body wants or has wanted Federal governmental agencies to succeed.

So, unless you are suddenly finding that you can in fact sustain some type of competitive work situation, when you get that initial denial or that reconsideration denial, don't think too deeply about it, don't even cry about it; *just appeal*.

I know you were waiting for a while for the decision and that you need the money *'yesterday'*, so to speak. I understand that. And yes, it sucks! A Lot!

In my article about the **Denial letter** (Item A. of your reading assignment above) I explained about how the denial letter is mostly a *"cookie-cutter"* letter with some paragraphs adapted to your case. Realize that these are letters sent to you hoping you simply accept their reasons for denial

To recap, people have to get very creative with their finances to support themselves during this time. But if you get a denial, giving up or stressing over it will not help you at all! *Health or otherwise.* Treat the first denial as part of the process.

Remember that *life goes on* and you may get approved in the next round or by a judge on the third round (*this varies by jurisdiction! Some States only have a total of two rounds, not three!*).

A lot of people simply don't follow through and give up after reading the disability denial letter.

Don't be one of those people!

I even tell my clients that they almost certainly *will* get denied on their first try. I know it is not very reassuring when someone seeks an attorney to move things along only to hear from that attorney that they are going to be denied. *"What am I hiring you for?"* is what folks may be understandably thinking. But please understand that even when you have an attorney, there is no guarantee of a *quick* win. And it may have nothing to do with the competency of the attorney. Very experienced attorneys *'lose'* these cases all the time. And some judges have a reputation for denying more cases than they should and doing it so often that the pattern becomes apparent in the *long-term* approval statistics that are kept for each judge.

As you can see, much of this is *'macro'* funding and political issue, that will only be changed by Congress or otherwise at the governmental level. Until then, we attorneys work with what we have and do our best to get results as quick as we can. *Why?*

One good reason: attorneys don't get paid *until* you win.

So, when an attorney tells their prospective client that they are going to lose the first round we know the battle is not over and success may well be on the way!

An analogy: have you heard the bit about scary flights? …*'when the stewardess panics, that's when you should panic'*. If an attorney is telling you not to panic over that first denial that means, it's not the time to panic!

I know what you're thinking, *"I'm panicking because of the money situation!"*

Yes, that is a valid reason for concern, which I hope the budgetary section of this book can at least help you with. I know the wait is brutal on the finances but once you win (*Positive thinking!*) you will have an accrued amount of back pay to catch up with the bills. No, it doesn't stop the bill-collector calls during that waiting period, but I want you to know that *it gets better.*

Now, on the second phase starting after you appeal that first denial, ...*i.e.*, what is called the *Reconsideration phase*[**], your chance of getting benefits increase a little more. Either because your evidence is good enough for them, or you finally retained an attorney who steered you toward just the right type of treatment and/or other evidence for an *'early'* win.

If you get denied after the *Reconsideration* period, you can appeal to request a hearing. And no, in jurisdictions (*States*) that have a reconsideration phase, you cannot skip ahead to the hearing phase. ... (a lot of folks ask me that!).

Unfortunately, you have to go through all the appeal levels available in your jurisdiction before you see a judge.

The hearing track is probably the most important phase in a disability case, as statistically, and by the processes that it involves, it affords the greatest chance of winning.

That's why I always urge people to not go it alone during this phase. Of course, it is not *impossible* to win at this phase without an attorney, but most people are not prepared for the work involved, and the surprises they are likely to run into at the hearing.

Many people go to the hearing hoping that somehow the evidence, *such as it is*, must surely somehow be enough. Others do not send any new evidence in during this phase and rely solely upon the fact that Social Security ordered records in the earlier phase(s) an/or mistakenly believe that the Hearing office

---

[**] Please check in your jurisdiction! Your State may not have this phase.

will order updated records as routinely as the State Agency offices did in the earlier phases.

The Hearing level comes after any reconsideration phase practiced by your jurisdiction (or in those jurisdictions without a reconsideration phase, after the initial phase). Once you request your hearing your file will leave the local office and will be sent to the ODAR (Office of Disability Adjudication and Review) *a.k.a.* "the Hearing Office".

This is the phase in which you will be seeing a judge in person or by video conference. More cases (*as a percentage of the total number considered at this phase*) are awarded in this phase than are awarded by the State Agencies (*relative to the total number that the State Agencies were processing*). Sadly, in some jurisdictions it can take a few years to be in front of the judge.

Beyond the Hearing phase, there are a couple more stages at which an appeal can continue, but complexity ramps up at those stages and I do not recommend claimants trying those on their own. Though admittedly the majority of attorneys do not extend their practice to appeals at these advanced stages. Nevertheless, you should at least try at those stages to see if you can find an attorney that can help!

To Recap:

If you get denied, appeal! ...No excuses and no giving up here.

Not my readers, at least!

C. How to Balance Your Budget Like A Pro

Living on a budget can be tricky and is even more so when your funds are limited to disability benefits.

The amount of monthly benefit a claimant gets if granted SSDI varies per person. It depends upon the number of *'earning quarters'* (Social Security tax) that the claimant has paid over the years, and (*to some extent*) which years those taxes were paid in, and the amount of the payments.

Either way, whether you have a bigger budget or a smaller budget there are things you can do to make your monthly expenses fit within that budget. You may find that you need to cut some extras here and there. And some of those cuts will be tough to make, so *fair warning!*

Keeping a budget when your income barely covers the *basics* can be a challenge

The first-time people sit down to do their budget after getting their first monthly benefit payment can be discouraging, to say the least. Good chance you're learning you cannot afford that old lifestyle anymore, maybe that nice house you worked so hard to get.

I hate that part of my job.

But I also did a fair amount of work as a Bankruptcy attorney, which routinely required me to deliver this type of difficult financial news. It was never fun, and this financial hardship aspect is something that will always be very difficult for me and my clients. But the reality is this:

Things change. ...very often!

Let's try to make the best of your awarded benefits: "Roof over your head, food on the table, a warm bed to sleep in".

You may be thinking: *"easy for you to say sitting there in your cushy job".* ...well, yes...and no.

I was not born and raised in a *cushy* setting. We never starved but money was very tight. I'm the oldest of Five kids. Anyone who has more than one kid knows: *Imagine 5!* So, I learned very early how to budget. And even now that things are a more stable financially, I still follow the same basic budget rules I grew up with.

Those budget rules are:

1. Don't buy any big-ticket items unless you *"really, really"* **need it!**

Does the old TV or car work? Is the couch old but still firm? If it's not *permanently broken*, you probably don't need a new one! If you simply get tired of an item, find ways to exchange, barter, upcycle, or recycle it.

I still own my 15-year-old couch! It's firm and the frame is still good. When the fabric got a little *tired-looking* a few years ago, I had it washed. Then I made a slip cover for it (paid $150 in fabric) and voila! *"New" couch with bragging rights!* I just saw a similar couch like mine with a similar slip cover worth $8000!

Who doesn't like a bargain!?

I'm not saying my couch is worth that much. But it's an example of how much in critical funds can be saved, and alternatively how much of those critical funds we can squander just because we have not thought through the impact to our budget of a pricey new replacement and perhaps have not thought through the ways in which to *repurpose* an existing item.

If you truly have the money, by all means, *buy it*!! …But if you are like most folks, we need to think more about creative ways to live on a tight budget. *And I want to show you that it can be done!*

2. If you don't have the money to pay in cash: *Don't buy it!*

Unless you are planning to pay off that card at the end of the month!

Credit cards are for *"super"* emergencies only (*e.g., someone died, and you need to fly somewhere last minute, and you didn't get paid your salary/benefit yet*). Credit cards should also *facilitate* your life (*buy things online or rental reservations*) and should not be used for splurges or 'impulse-buys', or for items that require multiple and protracted monthly credit-card payments.

That's how things get out of control! You buy minimally today with your card, you pay off that bill when it comes!

Use it, pay it off! Use it, pay it off!

This is major: By not spending on *"unneeded extras"* you hopefully don't unduly increase that credit card balance!

It's that simple!

By following this simple rule, you will be able to bring that balance down within your budget, even if you had a big last-minute expense. You can even start paying down your old cards by following this rule too. By not using the card, your balance will only increase by that interest rate but not by an unnecessary expense.

Old habits die hard

The reason I follow these rules is because I was brought up with a very *budget-conscious* mother. She made it possible to pay all the bills despite a tight budget. She was still able to find money here and there for a new outfit for the kids every 3 months or so. And as an adult, I still remember looking under the couch to find coins for the bus fare to go to school. But I managed and still found ways to go to school and graduate.

I realize the details of my own story may not be completely relevant to your budgeting efforts, but I want to express that *I know your struggle*.

That's why I want you to make it! And I want you to know that it is possible to live on a tight budget.

While I have been lucky so far, things can change for *me* too. Just like it did with you. I know it doesn't solve your budget problem here. But here is something else that is important to keep in mind:

Life is full of ups and downs

I still remember when my father was *"downsized"* a couple of times during my childhood and teenage years. I was *completely "broke"* during law school. And the first few years after I moved back to the U.S. were *pretty tight*. The only reason I survived was because of my budgeting skills I learned early on.

So, I have been there and know how hard it is!

If you are not prepared, life can "kick your butt" in ways never imagined

That's why I want to prepare you for this. And if you are already on a tight budget (*on benefits*) let's find a way you can live comfortably, to the greatest extent possible.

For ideas on how to survive while waiting on benefits and after, please check **http://realtactics4disabilityclaims.com/survive-financially-social-security-disability/**.

Now, this budget will bring certain realities to light. Some not as happy as you and I would like. But at least you will now what the reality is. From there you will be able to make informed decisions on what to do next. You may need to sell some extra things, downsize your home, downsize expenses, *etc.*

Downsizing

If you wish to start the process of downsizing, do a little research, read some blogs, *etc.*

For example, I have a friend, a fellow-blogger, who gives many helpful insights about minimalist living, including about how to downsize and to live within your means. You may consider checking out her blog at **www.chibeingchi.com/minimalist-blogs/2016/10/9/minimalist-made-stupid-easy**. I believe she offers a free *e-book* on downsizing tips.

Now that you have some basic information and references to look into, you can develop new methods that work for you and your family.

D. How to Create and Maintain a Budget Without Starving

The biggest issue most people have when trying to fit in a budget is not seeing *"the big picture"*.

The big picture is your income versus your budget. Once you have the big picture you will be able to *"see"* what kind of budget you will need to fit in.

Most people fit in four categories: *"Thrifty"* (or extremely thrifty), *"Thrifty but will splurge occasionally"*, *"The Big Spender"* and the *"Hoarder"*

Believe it or not, these categories have nothing to do with how much a person makes a month. These are simply *"behaviors"* defining your money-management. The "big spender" is not necessarily a millionaire and you can certainly have a millionaire who is extremely thrifty; *Ebenezer Scrooge, anyone?*

Before preparing a budget or even considering a budget you need to know what kind of money-manager you are and where you fit within these Four categories. *Be realistic and honest with yourself.* Not doing so will only prolong the challenges you are having with your budget.

Pretend you are going to an addicts meeting. Look at yourself in the mirror and say:

"Hi, my name is so and so and I'm a _____ (Insert your budget behavior here) ____."

No one needs to hear it but you. You can do this in the bathroom, in your bedroom, or in a forest. ...as long as *you* are listening.

Why Should You Be Asking the Budget Behavior Question?

If it is not apparent to you why you should know what type of budget behavior you are prone to good chance you are one of those folks who have a stack of bills and are panicking about what to do with them.

Budget-behavior, of course, varies widely from person to person:

Maybe you are someone who is having a *"guilt trip"* about that visit to Cancun that you are trying to set up. In a way this is useful for not overspending.

And maybe you are one of those folks who take savings to the next level and actually cannot let go of very minor things, such as a store clerk accidently shortchanging you a dollar or two, and you obsessively think about that for three days!

On the other hand, maybe you are someone who has to live paycheck to paycheck because you feel a need to acquire *'collectibles'*, ...but for *hoarding* rather than in a way that might produce a positive financial return.

For example, you buy things that you think are collectibles and sit on those for years, without looking into reselling them or even using them for any practical purpose (*boxed Superman toys, anyone?*).

The point is, different examples and types of financial wisdom and financial folly are almost endless and suffice it to say most people *should* be (*or should want to be*) in the *"thrifty but will splurge occasionally category"*.

Ideally, those in this category will know how much he/she makes and plan for the timely payment of bills and expenses; and ideally will have at least a little left for retirement savings and/or for unforeseen expense, including, *God forbid*, an emergency; and yet will also kind of keep it in perspective, and remember that because life is short to not go to budgeting extremes and be *miserly* with themselves or their loved ones and dependents.

The Extremely Thrifty

If you had an excellent salary when you worked but still count the number of toilet paper sheets you use when going to the bathroom, and that sort of thing, …then you are *extremely thrifty*. Perhaps too much so.

I know: …it's *your money* and you can do whatever you want with it. And as you've read here, I also agree that saving for a rainy day is an *excellent idea*. But it saddens me to think of people who are eating oatmeal for lunch and dinner to save money yet make six-figures a year!

This is a bit extreme.

Let's think real Big Picture here: In the end, you die, and unless you're saving it for worthy and loved family members, either *someone else will burn that money* really quick, or *it goes to the government*.

My point here is while a *well-run* budget is good, but don't neglect to enjoy at least some of the fruits of your labor ….so if you worked all year and lived tight to save money to go to Europe, please go to Europe!

The Big Spender

Quite a different character than the extremely thrifty, the big spender usually has an average salary that could give him/her a comfortable life but surrounds himself/herself by luxury he/she *can't afford*.

I once knew a person who lived in an 800 square foot apartment and had 3 TVs! *Oh,* and he didn't own them. *He rented them!!*

Who needs 3 TVs anyway? …and it was just him, it wasn't as if family members or roommates were using the TVs.

Another person I knew owned a Hummer and was a stay-at-home dad. He said he was pursuing an "acting career" (nothing wrong with a stay-at-home dad or having dreams). However, it was not ok to see his wife driving a *"beater"*. And she was working *two jobs* because they could not pay their bills including that big Hummer!

Really!?

Another characteristic of the big spender is high credit card debt and *nothing to show for it by a houseful or garage-full of quickly-depreciating items*. This is a person who buys a lot of trinkets, purses, and expensive things that lose value as soon as they leave the store.

The big spender also buys or *"needs"* to buy brand names only. The thought of buying some secondary brand is *"so-last-year"* for that person.

The Hoarder

Here's another *'extreme'* type. I'm not talking about examples you might have seen on TV, but some can certainly fit into that category...*i.e.*, innovatively successful like for example those "*American Pickers*" guys. ...Not those folks, they made a success of it. I'm talking about the *toy collector*, the *comics-collector*, the *car collector* who has 20 cars in various stages of restoration but continue to rust and take up space.

Or another example: the toy collector with a houseful of impulse purchases which he has no intention of trading or selling for profit, with much of his *'inventory'* not even really *'smart purchases'* from a collection standpoint.

Those situations where the collector doesn't *'restore'* the collected items, nor otherwise use them; where the items are taking up space in your yard or bookshelves and give *no joy or monetary recompense*.

And the most absurd part of it all, the hoarder often lives *paycheck-to-paycheck,* but are sometimes sitting on a *small fortune!*

Why not sell some items? Live better?

...have a small collection. Fine, ...but when you won't or can't even feed the dogs because of your collection, you have a problem! Sell some of that stuff that you know you will never use, restore or play with!

Finding Balance on Spending Behaviors

We all should strive to find balance in life. ...and in the financial realm that means avoid needless starvation on the one hand but avoid big spending on the other. You can have a comfortable life with very little and an uncomfortable life with a lot. So, strive for a middle ground.

Now that we hopefully have a better idea (*having read this section and done some self-reflection*) of who we are financially, it is time to create a budget so that we can at least find peace of mind knowing that we can *"make it"* to the end of the month.

The Bankruptcy Method of Budgeting *(hear me out!)*

I am going to show you how applying a *"bankruptcy"* method of creating a budget will put things into perspective when it comes to balancing your budget.

Oh, and I'm not saying you are bankrupt or that you will need to file for bankruptcy during this process (*...well, it may eventually come to that for some*). But this 'bankruptcy-budget' is eye-opening when you see how it works.

First, I need to explain the basic difference between the most common types of bankruptcies most people file, so you can understand what a tight budget is and what a more flexible budget is.

The Tightest form of Budgeting is applied to a Chapter 7 Bankruptcy

A Chapter 7 bankruptcy is the one where you eliminate all your debts (*with some exceptions and exemptions*). This is of course a very *"bare-bones"* explanation.

Now, to qualify for this type of bankruptcy there is a certain budget that the courts allow; namely when comparing your net income (*after taxes*) and your *expenses*, there cannot be any money left to spend *after* paying all your BASIC* bills. In short, that you are either at *zero or in the negative*.

That's how someone would fit in a Chapter 7: **There is no money left to pay creditors.**

If you find yourself in this situation after doing the Chapter 7 style budget, then it's time to tighten the belt ...*Something's gotta give!*

And the Chapter 7 style budget will likely reveal those areas you are spending too much on or where you are losing control on things.

Yes, I understand your salary simply may not cover everything. That's why we will talk about tightening your belt here ...*yes, even more!*

The Chapter 13 Budget

A Chapter 13 Bankruptcy is the type that you repay a portion of your debts, (*again with variations and lots of rules*).

In this type of budgeting, you have the money to pay all your BASIC* bills and there is some money left over.

If there's money left over, why would anyone need to file a Chapter 13?

That's where things get interesting and where a lot of people get into trouble. Yes, there is money to pay all the basic bills but not enough money to pay for credit cards and other *"splurges"*.

Such folks are simply *over-extended*.

This happens a lot with people using credit cards and come to find that they cannot even make the minimum payments. Specifically, in this situation the combination of your basic bills plus the minimum payments of credit cards eat all your income, and then some.

That's why folks will fit into this category. A Chapter 13 *"repayment-plan"* will allow *some* of the debts to be forgiven, but not all.

The Bankruptcy Budget Outline:

- **List all your earnings:** Salary (*after taxes*), rental income, overtime pay, etc. List any and every source of income. Then Compare those totals.

- **Outline all your BASIC* bills:** These are the *"bankruptcy budget"* acceptable bills (do not include credit cards here).

The BASIC* bills are:

- **Rent/Mortgage** (*does it include tax and Insurance?*): This should not exceed 35% of your salary

- **Utilities:** Water, electricity, gas, oil (*heating*), sewer, trash, telephone (*landline*) and cell phone.

- **Home Maintenance:** This only applies if you hire a gardener to clean your yard or mow the lawn every month or a pool person. It also applies for minor repairs around the house.

This is a place where you can cut costs. Do you really need a gardener? Can the kids help with the lawn?

- **Food:** This will vary per State - Some states have a very high cost of living. But this is another area that needs to be trimmed to BASIC necessities. Do you really need that candy or that expensive yogurt if you are trying to cut costs and make things fit within your salary?

    Notice that if you substitute some *'better'* foods for *"crappy foods"* you may spend less in the long run even though a box of generic mac-n-cheese for example costs less than, say, a bag of organic *'power-greens'*. There are health considerations with that change too. You eat better, very likely you end up spending less with doctors.

- **Clothing:** Do you buy clothes every month? If so, set a budget for the year and stick with it.

    For example: Say you select $80 a month for clothes. If you don't buy anything this month, now you have $160 for next month.

    If you budget it this way, you will see that you will have more money than you think and may even see that you don't need all that money to buy clothing. You may also find that you are spending way more than that amount in clothes per month (*or week!*), and that's why you are *"blowing"* your budget.

    Maybe visit outlet stores or consider *overstock* type stores. Stick with the basics to start: *classic (non-pricey) pants, shirts, underwear, socks, classic shoes*. Buy clothes that are *"neutral"* in style and that can be worn for years.

Save the brand-name stuff as an *extra* that you can only buy if you were *"good"* with the budget the month before ...meaning, you did not spend all of last month's allotment of the whole monthly clothing-budget.

And if you do not require some special business wardrobe, consider the basics for work clothes too: t-shirts, pants, socks, sweaters, basic shorts.

Do you really need a brand name? What you may buy for $50 is likely available for $15 somewhere else, simply because the less pricey version wasn't given the brand-name label. There is some evidence that the same production factories put different labels on some of the exact same products depending solely upon their buying-retailer.

- **Laundry and Dry Cleaning:** Do you wear a lot of suits? If so, consider ways to rotate them so you don't require weekly dry cleaning. For the ladies, maybe buy some classic pants that could be worn as separates with your suit jackets for example. *It's better for the environment too!*

- **Medical and Dental:** These can really do some *'damage'* to the budget unless you are insured, ...and nowadays even if you are insured, what with ever-increasing deductibles and out-of-pocket-minimum provisions in most health plans.

But just like a credit card minimum payment, those health insurance co-pays add up if you have a medical condition and need to be at the doctor frequently. If the time is right, consider revisiting your health plan to see if you can get a lower cost plan with better coverage for co-pays.

But generally, the lower the co-pays the higher that deductible is.

Same goes for the insurance monthly payments (even if you are partly covered by your employer). For the medical expense portion of your budget, be sure to include any out-of-pocket expenses such as co-pays, medications you need every month, and maintenance fees for braces for the kids, for example.

- **Transportation:** You need to list your average fuel consumption per month, and such extras as occasional oil changes, tire changes, *etc.*

- **Recreation:** this is a *"budget blower"* for sure! Cable, Internet, Magazines, Newspapers, clubs, your subscription channels.

- **TV options:** Do you really need all those channels? There are many *"cut-your-cable"* options out there nowadays.

- **Internet:** This one is almost like the air we breathe.

Consider having home internet and watching your usage of data on the cell phone. Sometimes we are *"LOL-ing"* too much when we are out and about, not realizing that we are paying for too much cell phone data that could be reduced if only we used that time to talk to people instead of staring at our phones.

I just *"blew"* my phone data recently because I went on a trip and used the phone's GPS for directions on a 5-hour round trip! *Yes, even 'Miss Budget' here messes it up sometimes!*

- **Insurance:** Health insurance, auto insurance. ...can you check for lower rates? I know, we put off doing these things and end up going for another year with the same plan and/or same carrier *"just because..."*).

  Life Insurance: (consider the 'whole-life' type that allows you to have access to it instead of term life where the money just goes away if you stop paying).

- **Taxes** (...*i.e.*, generated by the ongoing income of your working house-hold and/or family members): budget for monthly and/or quarterly tax payments if not directly deducted from wages.

- **Installments:** car payment (consider buying an older car that it's paid for). Remember that a new car loses value as soon as you drive it out of the lot!

  In recent years there has actually been a glut of excellent cars out there, at or below cost, for sale by private parties if you know where to look. But if you cannot afford to pay for one out-of-pocket then finance with your own bank instead wherever possible, particularly if you are buying from a commercial dealer.

  But if you can buy on the private market, you will likely be pleasantly surprised at how much money you can save. Plus, you don't have to deal with a car salesman pitch (*no offense if you are one*).

- **Alimony/child support:** another *"budget blower"*. But please pay your dues!

You don't want to end up in court. However, if your financial situation changed, *do not wait* until you are so far behind that now they are looking at wage garnishment.

That would certainly mess with your budget *big time*! Going to court may allow you to lower your payments and you will still be on time with your duties to your kid(s) and ex.

- **Payments to support others:** This can really mess with your budget.

That family member who is always in trouble and you frequently bail out him/her. Or your kid in college...current financial wisdom says do *not* pay out what would otherwise be your retirement funds for college expenses for your child. And that is because the paradigm of the *'value'* of higher education is rapidly changing in these days of on-line courses, *etc.*, and also because those student loan debts incurred by your child are currently not dischargeable in bankruptcy, and the commonly seen student-debt to prospective income ratio is rapidly deflating with the astronomical increases in tuition level these last several decades.

Your kid can and/or should work!

Even if it's just for a few hours a week to help out with some of their expenses. Think of it this way, if you had to work to survive college, they can too!

I know you want to be a good parent and help. But if you are not meeting your minimum payments just so your kid can go to *"Toga"* parties and only to earn a devaluing degree, then you may be signing on to a financial situation with severe and permanent consequences for you and your child.

Life is tough and if your child does not learn how to budget soon, they and you may wind up in terrible financial difficulty.

- **Expenses for your business:** if you are self-employed.

- **Miscellaneous expenses:** Set a budget for lipstick, nail polish, your latte. For the guys: buying tools or any other extras that you like: New pens, printing ink, *etc.*

  Make sure such expense items are *necessary* and that you will use them up *before* buying a new one... (I say this because I am myself addicted to buying mascaras! Long lashes, volume lashes, *you name it!* ...I need to improve on that for sure!)

- **Contributions for retirement:** This is important if you have any leftover money. If nothing is left, then cutting expenses would certainly allow you to start this.

  Even if it is $10 a month. Put it away in a retirement account (*consult your banker, of course*) and *"forget"* that money.

The list is extensive, but you can narrow it down to your situation and expenditures and take control of your expenses.

The *'bankruptcy method'* of budgeting follows the guidelines from the IRS. Believe it or not, the IRS has guidelines for expenses and there are other similar useful regulations that flow from which state you live in. If you make yourself aware of those particular tax and/or bankruptcy *'exemptions'* for the particular State that you live in, you can tailor your budget more closely to the cost-of-living exemptions in your State, which may actually be higher than the national average.

Here's the link to the IRS site at **https://www.irs.gov/businesses/small-businesses-self-employed/collection-financial-standards**.

Notice that the IRS budget is posted for *collection purposes*, yet you can use this as a guide if you are trying to fit into the *"bankruptcy budget"* I'm suggesting.

Don't forget that when doing a monthly budget, start with your last 6 months of expenses as a comparison.

That's the only way you will figure out how to average things out like electricity (hot months versus cold) or seasonal expenses.

For example: say you live in a warmer climate, such as Arizona; if during the Summer you use more AC and your bill is $400 a month for three months, but during the Winter it goes down to $100; then average it out by multiplying $400 x 3 and the average for the lower months and multiply that by 9.

So, if for the higher months the total is $1,200 (three or four hundred per month), but for the rest of the year it is $100 per month on the average, then add the $1200 for the three higher months to the $900 for the nine lower months. That comes to $2,100 a year divided out by the 12 months of the year = $175 per month.

That is, you should budget $175 a month for electricity.

The months that the bill is only $100 you set aside that $75. When the higher expense months come along, then you will have that money sitting there. You will be able to make ends meet when you get that $400 bill in the summer because you saved for it*.

*Some utility companies may offer budget plans to keep your bill *"fixed"* every month if you stay within *"usage"* limits (this varies by State).

The same calculation goes for every budgeted expense that you do not spend on every month, such as medical expenses or home repairs, car-tires, oil changes, *etc.*

I hope that you consider these tips to create and maintain a healthy budget for yourself and/or your household. You do not need to splurge all the time. Honestly, if you have a roof over your head, a warm bed, and food, *what else do we need*?

Checklist

To download my Super Nifty Checklist to keep track of your medical treatment, please go to **http://realtactics4disabilityclaims.com/checklist-pdf/**

You can print as many copies as needed to keep track of everything for the duration of your claim.

Please note that this is a copywritten material and you are only authorized to make copies for your own personal use. Do not share this material with others.

Made in the USA
Middletown, DE
02 May 2019